A Theology of Justice

A Theology of Justice

Interpreting John Rawls in Corrections Ethics - An Ethnography

LARRY DONELL COVIN JR.

Foreword by Marvin Crawford

WIPF & STOCK · Eugene, Oregon

A THEOLOGY OF JUSTICE
Interpreting John Rawls in Corrections Ethics - An Ethnography

Copyright © 2022 Larry Donell Covin Jr. All rights reserved. Except for brief quotations in critical publications or reviews, no part of this book may be reproduced in any manner without prior written permission from the publisher. Write: Permissions, Wipf and Stock Publishers, 199 W. 8th Ave., Suite 3, Eugene, OR 97401.

Wipf & Stock
An Imprint of Wipf and Stock Publishers
199 W. 8th Ave., Suite 3
Eugene, OR 97401

www.wipfandstock.com

PAPERBACK ISBN: 978-1-6667-3881-0
HARDCOVER ISBN: 978-1-6667-3882-7
EBOOK ISBN: 978-1-6667-9994-1

JUNE 8, 2022 3:22 PM

Contents

Foreword by Marvin Crawford | vii

Acknowledgements | xi

Introduction: A Theology of Justice Corrections Ethics | xiii

Chapter 1 Theological Arguments in Conversation with Law and Social Contract Theory | 1

Chapter 2 John Rawls and Social Contract Theory Concepts | 26

Chapter 3 A History of Corrections in the United States | 34

Chapter 4 Social Contract Theory as a Basis for a Corrections Ethic | 59

Chapter 5 Environmental Factors Leading to Jail and Prison | 70

Chapter 6 Individual Agency and Incarceration | 92

Chapter 7 Treatment versus Security | 104

Bibliography | 121

Index | 127

Foreword

Let Our Hands Move to Heal
Let God's People Live
O'er The Land, O'er the sea
Healing Will Be for You and Me
Let Our Hands Move to Heal

It is with deep appreciation and ineffable enthusiasm that I have the opportunity to write the foreword in Dr. Larry Covin's book *A Theology of Justice*, which provides an ethical and theological platform, to address one of our nation's continued and harshest sins of colonial slavery—the criminalization and mass incarceration of the poor, the mentally ill, black boys, black men, and, unfortunately, in increasing numbers, poor women of color. Poor communities and communities of color have carried a disproportional burden of this "slavery by another name" in all aspects of their lives, including healthcare, voting rights, sexually transmitted diseases, violence, etc. I applaud Dr. Covin for wrestling with the ethical paradigms to bring about justice in the penal system and save at-risk communities and people from America's vicious and nefarious criminal justice system.

My exposure to the incarcerated over the years has been primarily in an indigent healthcare setting where I provide and teach medicine, and in the church/community setting where I raise

Foreword

funds and find lawyers to defend my brothers and sisters of color from oppressed communities. I started my career as a physician with Morehouse School of Medicine in Atlanta, Georgia, at Grady Memorial Hospital with the noble intent to serve the underserved. I have been with institution for thirty years and, by the nature of the patient population, I fulfill that vision daily as clinical professor and undergrad medical education administrator. One of the saddest and most challenging aspects of providing care in this setting is the prison population. The prisoners are often young and vibrant or older repeat offenders shackled physically and emotionally. Their education achievements were much below their abilities and, more times than not, imprisoned for small infractions of the law and had no direct legal defense contacts except for the day of the trial. Their mental illnesses have never been addressed properly which could have prevented their incarceration or been part of their defense. The physical complaints were numerous, ranging from chronic diseases prevalent among the poor to sexually transmitted diseases associated directly with incarceration. From the early days of my practice and pastorate, I saw firsthand mass incarceration destroying the very essence of the incarcerated.

A letter addressing the By These Healing Hands ceremony at Morehouse School of Medicine in May of 2015 sums up my thoughts of the problem from a healthcare perspective:

> This year our ceremony is dedicated to highlighting the healthcare disparities arising from police brutality against economically challenged communities and mass incarceration . . . the injustices of the prison population being 40% black males, although they are only 6% of the population, and the rising number of African American women who are being imprisoned for petty drug violations at 4.8 times the rate of white women adds another dimension of healthcare disparities associated with unfair sentencing and cruel punishment while incarcerated. The young(juveniles) often suffer from "psycho-trauma" if placed in isolation; the repeated African American male offender spreads HIV between the community and prison population; and the unfortunate raping of

Foreword

incarcerated women who are further punished with solitary confinement if they file a complaint. These are the healthcare disparities born of mass incarceration and police brutality that must be addressed by the religious, political, social, and medical communities through the eyes of compassion if we are to mend the wounds of the broken and maintain these United States of America.

Dr. Covin sets the groundwork to further address and resolve unjust criminalization and incarceration.

Dr. Larry Covin is one of the significant African American human rights theologians and liberation theology theologians in America, and, I dare say, soon to be across the world. His writings can be found in the libraries of more than a hundred colleges and universities across America, including Harvard University, Princeton University, Princeton Theological Seminary, Stanford University, University of California at Berkeley, Columbia University, Notre Dame, University of Chicago, Howard University, Atlanta University, Emory University, and the University of Georgia.

He is in fact what Antonio Gramsci refers to as *Organic Intellectual*, writing from his space as the systematic theologian-religion scholar at Historic Trinity UCC Church (1742) in York, Pennsylvania.

We first met as students at Albany State College in the 1980s where he majored in criminal justice and was an ROTC cadet. He went on to earn the Master of Divinity from the Interdenominational Theological Center, the Doctor of Ministry from the Lancaster Theological Seminary at Moravian University, and a Postdoctoral ThM degree in theology and ethics from Princeton Theological Seminary.

He is the author of *Thirteen Turns: A Theology Resurrected From the Gallows of Jim Crow Christianity*. In his latest book, *A Theology of Justice: Interpreting John Rawls in Corrections Ethics ~ An Ethnography*, Dr. Covin has created a comprehensive corrections ethic for jails and prisons in the United States.

This latest book should be a must-read for every university student, NGO human rights watch group, faith-based organization,

Foreword

seminarian, and others to learn how to make complex theological and ethical thoughts practical. Dr. Covin has perfected the art of addressing the "-isms" in the context of classical and contemporary thinkers while remaining faithful to scholarship as he critiques issues of the oppressed. His extensive experience in the correctional system and military gives him a distinctive edge over his contemporaries to apply and create ethical thoughts in the context of prison and jail life. He marries the practical to the scholarship, compassion to passion, and the heart to the mind. He draws us into the hidden injustices parading as law, order, decency, and acceptability, then makes us ask, "Why is this?" He leads us from "*theo-doxis* to *theo-praxis*."

> Let our tender hearts broken masses feel
> Then compassion let us daily live
> Open eyes to see deep care
> Reveal our sacred skills to share

Dr. Marvin L. Crawford, MD, MDiv

Acknowledgements

A Theology of Justice: Interpreting John Rawls in Corrections Ethics ~ An Ethnography, reflects over twenty years of research. This project began as a research project, as my doctoral dissertation at The Lancaster Theological Seminary at Moravian University; and yet another iteration with brief excerpts appearing in a journal article titled, *Homelessness, Poverty, and Incarceration: The Criminalization of Despair.* Finally, the book that has emerged as *A Theology of Justice*, while possessing the DNA of these renditions, is my magnum opus, and the emerging work is unique, to comparable commentaries on the criminal justice system encompassing jails and prisons in the United States. Thus, a corrections ethic for jails and prisons.

Thank you to my alma maters that educated me and enlightened me. Albany State University (BS), The Interdenominational Theological Center (MDiv), The Lancaster Theological Seminary at Moravian University (DMin), Princeton Theological Seminary (ThM).

Thank you to my congregation where I serve as Systematic Theologian-Religion Scholar, at Historic Trinity UCC Church (1742) in York, Pennsylvania.

Thank you to my publisher Wipf & Stock for their continued collaboration. Together, we have published *Thirteen Turns: A Theology Resurrected from the Gallows of Jim Crow Christianity* in 2020, and *A Theology of Justice* in 2022.

Acknowledgements

I am eternally grateful to those who are responsible for my development over the years. First, to my late parents, Isabelle Brown Covin and Larry Donell Covin Sr., for nurturing me and creating an environment in which I could flourish. To my paternal grandfather Rev. Roger Lee Brown, who would serve as my first theology professor, as I listened to his teaching from his pulpit of over forty years. To my favorite uncle, Dr. Trevor D'Broun, ESQ—affectionately known as Uncle T—who was an autodidact teaching himself to read, before being admitted to university and eventually law school. To my wife and children: Gloria, Nicholas, Roger, Larry III, and Joel. We are so proud of our sons.

Finally, to all of the unsung members of the village, in Long Branch and Neptune, New Jersey, most of whom never enjoyed the privilege of graduating from high school, and certainly never visited a college campus, who participated in mentoring me, nurturing me, watching over me, and encouraging me. I cannot name each one of you, however, you continue to watch over me as part of that *Great Cloud of Witnesses*.

I hope that my work has made you proud. I love you.
Thank you.

Dr. Larry Donell Covin Jr.
aka "The Governor"

INTRODUCTION
A Theology of Justice Corrections Ethics

THERE ARE THIRTY EIGHT ethical statements/principles throughout the seven chapters of *A Theology of Justice*. These ethical statements as a whole form a comprehensive corrections ethic informed by the human rights abuses occurring in jails and prisons within the United States, offering evidence-based correctives. This corrections ethic is informed by twenty years of qualitative research inside four jail and prison institutions, as an administrator of both treatment and religious services departments; including the United States Disciplinary Barracks at Leavenworth, United States Penitentiary in Atlanta, Maryland Division of Pretrial Detention and Services in Baltimore, Maryland, and the Adams County Adult Correctional Complex in Gettysburg, Pennsylvania.

These ethical statements/principles may be studied prior to reading *A Theology of Justice*, and serve as a stand-alone correctional ethics Bill of Rights as well.

As you read each corrections ethic in the context of each chapter, the ethic will accomplish greater impact as it is informed with both context and demonstration of its praxis.

> I. *Corrections Ethic One*—True jail and prison reform must be instigated by persons external to the administration of jails and prisons. It is not possible to be a prison reformer from the inside. The restraints and pressure for self-preservation, ultimately will be too enormous to

Introduction

enact the kind of change that qualifies for jail and prison reformation. Those inside the jails and prisons can do well and act humanely; however, far-reaching prison reform must be done by those who are not impacted by the fear of reprisal by jail and prison officials. Jail and prison reform must be done from the outside. This is true not only for jail and prison employees but ex-offenders as well.

II. *Corrections Ethic Two*—An effective corrections ethic must have as its litmus test what John Rawls refers to as *reflective equilibrium*. One is unable to achieve reflective equilibrium as an official within the jail or prison. It is not until an official is outside of the system, that he or she can reflect accurately, upon the policy and procedure mechanisms governing correctional institutions, and give useful feedback in order to inform the aforementioned policy and procedure mechanisms.

III. *Corrections Ethic Three*—An effective corrections ethic should have as a requirement the incorporation of education programming into the goals and measures of inmate treatment plans. Inmate treatment plans outline the strategies and guidelines to be followed by clinicians in treating inmates. Evidenced-based, pedagogically informed curricula that emphasizes skills focusing upon healthy relationships, relative to parenting and other family dynamics, are essential to a corrections ethic.

IV. *Corrections Ethic Four*—An effective corrections ethic must have as a central goal an emphasis on understanding the uniqueness of the individual, or even groups, of highly difficult inmate populations. A thorough diagnosis, during the intake process, to include classification and treatment planning, of not only the *Presenting Problem* but the origin of their behavioral problems, will give substantive and substantial insight relative to responding to inmate delinquency and malfeasance.

Introduction

V. *Corrections Ethic Five*—An effective corrections ethic must take into account those lacking the requisite *natural assets* to function in society, and to function within the rules and regulations of jails and prisons.

VI. *Corrections Ethic Six*—John Rawls posits that the foremost characteristic of a social institution should be the concern of *just* institutions. Institutions such as the correctional facilities which make up jails and prisons in the United States should incorporate a humane corrections ethic into its culture through jail and prison policy and procedure mechanisms. The social contract theory as espoused by John Rawls in *A Theory of Justice* conceptualizes how a just society and just institutions would function through the introduction of many of its principles.

VII. *Corrections Ethic Seven*—An attainable corrections ethic must be grounded in realistic and achievable goals, empirical and measurable, which not only critique the present state of conditions within jails and prisons, but offer measurable and implementable alternatives.

VIII. *Corrections Ethic Eight*—An effective corrections ethic must take into consideration those *Scattered Individuals* in society and create contingencies for their control.

IX. *Corrections Ethic Nine*—Corrections ethics must acknowledge both the necessity of disproportionality of power in jails and prisons, as well as the inherent abuses that disproportionality inherently brings. The remedy of this conundrum is found in what Rawls refers to as the *difference principle* in *A Theory of Justice*. The difference principle recognizes and even affirms the inequity in societal arrangements, and that individuals and groups will always find themselves either on the top or bottom strata of society. The difference principle, however, emphasizes that those in positions of power in society are justified in

Introduction

enjoying their standing if in fact *their good fortune* is to the benefit of the larger society as a whole.

X. Corrections Ethic Ten—An effective corrections ethic then must justify the power distribution in jails and prisons, as a means to empower inmates through rehabilitative programming and treatment, during their incarceration, as a means to reduce recidivism and facilitate re-entry into society.

XI. *Corrections Ethic Eleven*—An effective corrections ethic must affirm that private, for-profit jails and prisons make their profit on the incarceration of men, women, and children. If their numbers are increased, and the inmate population rises, then private and for-profit jails and prisons secure their profitability. When prison numbers are decreased, it is a threat to the viability and sustainability of the private, for-profit, jail and prison economic model. Treatment, and rehabilitative programming, are designed to decrease recidivism and reintegrate the offender back into mainstream society. The attrition of offenders exiting the system of incarceration diminishes the profit of private, for-profit, jails and prisons.

XII. *Corrections Ethic Twelve*—An effective corrections ethic must be capable of deconstructing the systematic network of institutions, practices, and perceptions that perpetuate dysfunctional, traumatized, and criminogenic persons and communities.

XIII. *Corrections Ethic Thirteen*—An effective corrections ethic must take seriously the assertion by Jean-Jacques Rousseau that *slaves lose everything in their chains, even the desire of escaping from them.* Therefore an effective corrections ethic must devise through curricula, or other pedagogical instruments, and through therapeutic modalities, effective strategies for elucidating the phenomenon known as *internalized racist oppression*.

Introduction

XIV. *Corrections Ethic Fourteen*—An effective corrections ethic must affirm that the for-profit, prison privatization, prison industrial complex views human beings as commodities, or in social contract parlance *as means* to financial profitability, and not *as ends* toward personhood and dignity.

XV. *Corrections Ethic Fifteen*—An effective corrections ethic must begin with an articulation of its rudimentary conception, of the essential character of persons relative to their potential for possessing the *Capacity for Moral Personality*. This conception of the essential character of persons then should inform the policies and procedures, standard operating procedures, treatment and rehabilitative modalities for jails and prisons.

XVI. *Corrections Ethic Sixteen*—An effective corrections ethic does not define the essential character of the inmate predicated upon the crime committed-no matter how heinous. An effective corrections ethic distinguishes between the essential character of the inmate, and the act or crime committed by the inmate.

XVII. *Corrections Ethic Seventeen*—An effective corrections ethic does not imply that treatment or rehabilitation is the absence of punishment. Treatment and punishment are coterminous, as long as the object of punishment serves to facilitate corrective behaviors, and not as a means to exact revenge upon the offender. The motivation informing the punishment is just as important as the imposing of punitive measures in an effective corrections ethic.

XVIII. *Corrections Ethic Eighteen*—An effective corrections ethic affirms the essential belief that individuals are capable of reform or rehabilitation, from criminogenic tendencies inculcated through their environment. Offenders are able to develop behaviors and skills through comprehensive education curricula, and therapeutic

Introduction

modalities in order to be successfully reintegrated into the community, or able to achieve the least restrictive security classification; ranging from maximum security classification, to a medium security classification, to a minimum security classification, to finally reintegration into the community in an *aftercare* model.

XIX. *Corrections Ethic Nineteen*—An effective corrections ethic interprets the correlation between disparities in wealth, or what Rawls refers to as *primary goods*, and the dissolution of order or civility within society, to the extent that individuals are excluded from participating in upward mobility, and the quality of life certain others are readily afforded due to the advantage of social location. The resulting effect of this debilitating correlation is the criminalization of entire communities and the branding of its citizens, African American youth in particular, as outlaws.

XX. *Corrections Ethic Twenty*—An effective corrections ethic corroborates the theories posited by both Jean-Jacques Rousseau and John Rawls, and the implications that social stratification portends, creates, and maintains a permanent underclass and jail and prison population, through the systematic implementation of policies, rules, and regulations, which serve as hegemonic strategies that erode the quality of life, dignity, and ethical judgment of *racialized communities.*

XXI. *Corrections Ethic Twenty-One*—An effective corrections ethic must analyze and incorporate into programs, curricula, policies, and procedures, and standard operating procedures, a methodology that interprets the context-ethos of environmental factors that lead to jail and prison.

XXII. *Corrections Ethic Twenty-Two*—An effective corrections ethic deconstructs the pathologies associated with the fracture of the family unit, and the criminogenic

Introduction

lifestyle internalized through the *succession of generations*, and the resultant contributing factors leading to the criminalization of individuals and whole communities.

XXIII. *Corrections Ethic Twenty-Three*—The *Morality of Association* refers to the community of which an individual is most influenced subsequent to the family. Because individuals do not exist in a vacuum, the influence of the environment upon the behavior of the individual cannot be overstated. The case can be made arguably that the societal norms and mores of a given community, can supersede even the influence of familial structures. Therefore, corrections ethics must advocate for intervention in the communities most severely affected by criminogenic patterns prior to, throughout, and post-incarceration.

XXIV. *Corrections Ethic Twenty-Four*—An effective corrections ethic must devise methodologies, mechanisms centered not on helping individuals to escape the so-called ghettos, or communities mired in despair for the suburbs, as this is not pragmatic; however, the goal must be to inundate communities with evidence based collaborations.

XXV. *Corrections Ethic Twenty-Five*—An effective corrections ethic should incorporate the Therapeutic Community or TC model, methadone as a viable alternative to heroin addiction, and spiritual practices as treatment modalities available to offenders and ex-offenders.

XXVI. *Corrections Ethic Twenty-Six*—An effective corrections ethic must astutely intervene in the recidivistic cycle of addiction and criminality. Laws enacted which criminalize individuals for nonviolent crimes committed as a result of their addiction, fail to address the complexity of human behavior and addiction. The addicted offender is not deterred by harsh sentences and the enactment of such rules and laws; the continued introduction of such is evidence that too many lawmakers either gain

Introduction

political capital from the perception of *get tough on crime* legislative agendas, or fail to comprehend the correlative relationships between addiction and criminality.

XXVII. *Corections Ethic Twenty-Seven*—An effective corrections ethic prioritizes the intervention in the recidivistic cycle of addiction and criminality, through the petitioning for drug courts throughout the country, and especially in communities most adversely affected by drug and alcohol addiction.

XXVIII. *Corrections Ethic Twenty-Eight*—An effective corrections ethic must deny the role of evil as a metaphysical reality informing criminogenic behavior. Utilizing the understanding of evil as defined by Dr. Philip Zimbardo, as existing due to *situation factors and social dynamics*, is a more pragmatic approach in interpreting heinous criminal acts. The danger of classifying certain inmate offenders as evil, in a metaphysical construct, is that it disavows the theoretical underpinnings of rehabilitation and treatment, and serves as antecedent to capital punishment.

XXIX. *Corrections Ethic Twenty-Nine*—An effective corrections ethic must courageously oppose the theoretical premise of capital punishment, although to do so is counterintuitive for many, including this author, and seemingly cathartic for society, when considered in the context of the most egregious acts against humanity. The premise of capital punishment suggests that there are certain human beings who are beyond redemption or rehabilitation. While there are offenders who are not within the capacity for rehabilitation to the extent they can live within society, an effective corrections ethic reaffirms the capacity for rehabilitation, to the extent that the vilest offenders are capable of existing within the custody of government conducted correctional facilities. The rights to life for

Introduction

criminals and law-abiding citizens alike are *erga omnes* rights and should be considered non-derogable rights.

XXX. *Corrections Ethic Thirty*—An effective corrections ethic reconciles the necessity for the coexistence of both custody and treatment pertaining to the sex offender. The need for strict custodial control is motivated less by the need for punishment, and more by the need for protecting society while simultaneously treating the sex offender. Due to the particularly revolting nature of this offense, correctional officials need to be vigilant addressing and responding to the offender, while affirming the humanity of the offender, and not defining the offender by the crime committed.

XXXI. *Corrections Ethic Thirty-One*—An effective corrections ethic must be implemented with impartial deliberateness, and avoid the compulsion to respond emotionally. It is improbable that corrections ethics would be adhered to by persons personally affected as victims of crime. If the tenets of corrections ethics are not established with foresight, behind a *veil of ignorance,* crafted with *maximin,* in the *original position,* and predetermined prior to established bias, or personal loss as a result of crime, the parameters and intent of a thoughtful corrections ethic may appear untenable.

XXXII. *Corrections Ethic Thirty-Two*—An effective corrections ethic must be conceived by those in the *original position* behind a *veil of ignorance.* Although by necessity jails and prisons must exist, the architects of treatment and rehabilitation, corrections officials, courts and judges, and societal attitudes should envision or conceptualize jails and prisons with the *maximin* as the guiding principle. In the context of corrections, the original position should consist of those who do not profit from the proliferation of jails and prisons, such as correctional entrepreneurial-privatization corporations, elected officials, contractual

Introduction

vendors such as medical providers, telecommunications networks, and refectory suppliers of inmate commissary accounts and meals, all of which have invested interest in the proliferation and human stocking of jails and prisons. The primary architects within the original position should be individuals and organizations, comprised of the following independent entities, or entities with similar constitutions and goals. Some of which are The Pennsylvania Prison Society, Amnesty International USA, Solitary Watch, Prison Watch Network, ACLU National Prison Project, and the United Nations Standard Minimum Rules for the Treatment of Prisoners.

XXXIII. *Corrections Ethic Thirty-Three*—An effective corrections ethic emphasizes the lack of agency or free will among the seriously mentally ill offenders in jails and prisons when lacking proper treatment measures. When offenders present with serious mental illness, they are clearly acting as those lacking the *capacity for moral personality*. Jail and prison policies and procedures, standard operating procedures, and mechanisms must require that all punitive measures against the seriously mentally ill offender be in consultation with institutional mental health providers. Wardens, commissioners, and correctional officials must be required to document and make available for public review confinement decisions affecting mentally ill offenders.

XXXIV. *Corrections Ethic Thirty-Four*—An effective corrections ethic advocates for enforcing punitive measures on not only predatory inmates, but also on correctional officers and institutional staff who fail to protect inmates or report jail and prison rape. A jail or prison, and correctional officials complicit in the culture of jail or prison rape, must be held liable for criminal prosecution in a court of law. Correctional officials should not have

Introduction

immunity from criminal prosecution in the case of jail and prison rape. Jail and prison rape is preventable.

XXXV. *Corrections Ethic Thirty Five*—An effective corrections ethic requires jails and prisons to make transparent their policies and procedures, standard operating procedures, mechanisms, and inmate medical requests, relative to the medical facilities and clinics operating within correctional facilities. This includes oversight by outside regulatory or oversight committees composed of medical professionals, medical ethicists, and concerned citizen groups. A contributing factor of medical malpractice, in correctional medical facilities and clinics, is the ability to operate clandestinely. Transparency within medical facilities and clinics facilitates the *health and vigor*, and the *self-respect* of the inmate population as defined in Rawlsian thought.

XXXVI. *Corrections Ethic Thirty-Six*—An effective corrections ethic affirms that security personnel and treatment staff are equally responsible for jail and prison conditions, which minimize the possibility of inmate suicide. Policies and procedures, standard operating procedures, inmate handbooks, mechanisms, and annual training of correctional employees must ensure that both security and treatment personnel are properly trained to recognize the warning signs of suicidal inmates. Correctional employees charged with safeguarding vulnerable or at-risk inmates who commit suicide must be subject to a full review of job performance to evaluate adherence to, or noncompliance with, suicide risk-management procedures.

XXXVII. *Corrections Ethic Thirty-Seven*—An effective corrections ethic requires civic organizations, religious organizations, and nonprofit organizations within the community, in solidarity—to eradicate the widespread use of jails and prisons, through due diligence in educating

Introduction

themselves on the available alternatives to jail and prison. The black church in particular, so dramatically impacted by jails and prisons, is recommended to create within its organization an alternative sentencing commission or auxiliary, as part of its programming. For our purposes, I will refer to this as the Paul and Silas Alternative Sentencing Initiative, or PASASI. These alternative sentencing options are provided here.

1. Drug Courts
2. Diversion Programs
3. Deferred Sentencing Programs
4. Restorative Justice
5. Home Detention
6. Weekend Jail Program
7. Work Release Program
8. Community Service Program
9. Electronic Monitoring Program
10. Sober Living Environment Program
11. Day Reporting Centers
12. Intensive Probation Supervision (IPS) Program

XIII. *Corrections Ethic Thirty-Eight*—An effective corrections ethic, as a final alternative sentencing mechanism, has at its disposal the use of the *individual's right to petition* the United Nations, for redress of human rights violations. W. E. B. Du Bois in conjunction with the NAACP made use of this mechanism in October of 1947, in order to bring attention to the violations of negroes' human rights in the United States, by the United States government. It is imperative that persons of color consider the individual's right to petition the United Nations, as a mechanism for redress of human rights violations resulting from jail and

Introduction

prison abuses. With the politicization and ever-increasing partisanship of our judicial system, marginalized communities have an alternative means to pursue justice: the individual's right to petition the United Nations.

- *Office of the United Nations High Commissioner for Human Rights—OHCHR "Complaints Procedures"*

Chapter 1

THEOLOGICAL ARGUMENTS IN CONVERSATION WITH LAW AND SOCIAL CONTRACT THEORY

SETTING THE STAGE—LIFE INSIDE TWO CORRECTIONAL FACILITIES

"THE CONDITIONS OF JAILS and prisons in the United States are more often than not deplorable and hidden from public view. The inhumane treatment of prisoners and their appalling living conditions are untenable and require justice."[1]

This book explores the ways in which John Rawls's *A Theory of Justice* may be used to construct a corrections ethic, in the context of jail and prison culture for correctional facilities in the United States. The chapters consider the varied and complex challenges faced while attempting the humane treatment of those incarcerated. The tradition of social contract theory espoused in the writings of such political philosophers as Thomas Hobbes, John Locke, Jean-Jacques Rousseau, and more recently amplified

1. Covin, "Homelessness, Poverty, and Incarceration," abstract.

in the work of Harvard political philosopher John Rawls, as well as the humanitarian emphasis in the teachings of didactic literature espoused in the Hebrew Bible and New Testament literature, will be explored and interpreted. Thus, this book creates a foundation for the creation of a corrections ethic grounded in social contract theory, undergirded by justice theory.

Writing in *A Theory of Justice* political philosopher John Rawls posits that institutions must prioritize justice even above efficiency. "Justice is the first virtue of social institutions, as truth is of systems of thought. A theory however elegant and economical must be rejected or revised if it is untrue; likewise laws and institutions no matter how efficient and well-arranged must be reformed or abolished if they are unjust."[2]

Within the context of Old Testament literature, the emphasis placed upon justice for the marginalized and the most vulnerable in community is unequivocal. Political philosopher and theologian Nicholas Wolterstorff, writing in *Educating for Shalom*, illuminates this concern. "The Old Testament declarations about justice is the passionate insistence that all the members of the community are entitled to a full and secure place in the life of the community. Hence the clanging repetitive reference to orphans, widows and sojourner."[3]

Justice. Ulpian, the Roman Jurist, expands upon the construct of justice, its conceptualization, and its application for the individual within the social contract. Writing in *Law and Theology: Classic Questions And Contemporary Perspectives*, David W. Opderbeck observes the following concerning justice. Opderbeck writes,

> As Christian philosopher Nicholas Wolterstorff notes in his magnificent book *Justice in Love*, "Doing justice is an example of love. Moses does not pit love and justice against each other." Wolterstorff cites the famous definition of "justice" from the Roman jurist Ulpian, found in Justinian's *Digest*. Ulpian said justice "is an enduring will

2. Rawls, *Theory of Justice*, 3.
3. Wolterstorff, *Educating for Shalom*, 143.

Theological Arguments in Conversation

to render to each his or her due." When we hear this definition, we usually think first of retribution: someone has done wrong, and what they are due is punishment. But as Wolterstorff notes, Ulpian's Latin speaks of rendering each person his or her *ius*—that is, his or her *right*.[4]

Justice for the imprisoned within our society, must be grounded in moral reasoning and undergirded by theological underpinnings. The negation of either *positive rights* or *negative rights* of occupants of the social contract, is an infringement upon not only the marginalized and the oppressed; however, upon humanity as a whole.

Immanuel Kant elucidates this claim. "Immanuel Kant (1724–1804), who emphasized the ethical responsibility to defend the dignity and worth of all people and declared in one of his most celebrated statements: Because a . . . community widely prevails among the Earth's peoples, a transgression of rights in one place in the world is felt everywhere."[5]

The justice motif in Old Testament writing echoes Immanuel Kant, and is evident in Ps 82:3 (NIV), "Defend the weak and the fatherless, uphold the cause of the poor and the oppressed."[6]

Reinhold Niebuhr postulates that a given society can be interpreted as to its valuation of justice, through an examination of how it engages its poor and marginalized in society. Writing in *Moral Man and Immoral Society*, Niebuhr makes clear; "The justice of a community is measured by its treatment of the powerless in society."[7]

Karl Barth, writing in *The Church Must Stand For Social Justice*, instructs us that the responsibility for the poor is not a tangential responsibility of the church; however, a primary focus of its mission. "The Church must concentrate first on the lower and lowest levels of human society. The poor, the socially and economically weak and threatened, will always be the object of its

---

4. Opderbeck, *Law and Theology*, 121–22.
5. Shelton, *Oxford Handbook*, 185.
6. Ps 82:3 (NIV)
7. Niebuhr, *Moral Man and Immoral Society*, 237.

primary and particular concern, and it will always insist on the State's special responsibility for these weaker members of society."[8]

Why then should devout persons, people concerned with the social contract, or those who observe Christianity, Islam, or Judaism devote the resources of time and energy to the plight of the incarcerated? To the most disdained elements of our society? Rabbi Abraham Joshua Heschel, who authored *Man Is Not Alone* and *God in Search of Man*, wrote famously of the interconnectedness of all humanity. This is sufficient evidence of our need to concern ourselves then with marginalized persons constitutive of jails and prisons.

> Abraham Joshua Heschel was a Jewish theologian and philosopher with a social consciousness that led him to participate in the civil rights movement. Considered "one of the truly great men" of his day and a "great prophet" by Martin Luther King, Jr., Heschel articulated to many Jewish Americans and African Americans the notion that they had a responsibility for each other's liberation and for the plight of all suffering fellow humans around the world.[9]

For Rabbi Abraham Joshua Heschel, the inference in my theological hermeneutic is that through working toward the liberation of *The Other*, we work toward our own freedom and liberation. The Other is salient in the ontological affirmation of the worth of societal's persons of none worth; the prostitute, the poor, the powerless, the disabled, in the teachings of Jesus in the New Testament text.

The false constructs, the manmade constructs which create fissures within society/race, royalty, entitlement, class, privilege, and conceptualizations that distort our human connectedness and *compassio*; the lack of a sense of connectedness therefore creates spaces for making The Other invisible. It is then possible to tolerate human rights abuses and atrocities. Thomas Merton, the Trappist monk, recalls his awakening in his journal *Conjectures of a Guilty*

---

8. Barth, *Christian Community and the Civil Community*, 173.
9. "Heschel, Abraham Joshua," para. 1.

Theological Arguments in Conversation

Bystander. "In Louisville, at the corner of Fourth and Walnut, in the center of the shopping district, I was suddenly overwhelmed with the realization that I loved all these people, that they were mine and I theirs, that we could not be alien to one another even though we were total strangers."[10] With the dismantling of these false constructs we are able to identify with, and therefore internalize, the *second great commandment.* "And the second is like it: 'Love your neighbor as yourself.' All the Law and the Prophets hang on these two commandments."[11] The most despised inmate is our neighbor.

David Opderbeck, again in *Law and Theology*, provides the historic groundwork for focusing upon this jail and prison demographic. Opderbeck outlines,

> The Bible is "full of legal material." This includes, for example, the specifically legal texts in the Torah, reflections on law and justice in the prophetic and wisdom literature, the summations of the law in Jesus's teaching, particularly in the Sermon on the Mount, the moral exhortations (*paraenesis*) in Paul's epistles, and further wisdom and prophetic reflections on law and justice in New Testament wisdom texts, such as James and Hebrews, and in apocalyptic texts, including Revelation. Various parts of these biblical texts have been central to religious and social life in the Christian West, the Islamic world, and the Jewish diaspora, and through that influence have directly impacted ideas about law and justice in Western and Arab civilizations since antiquity. As biblical scholar Brent Strawn has noted, "It does not seem to be going too far to say that all of the Bible is—or have been or could be—law, even if only (!) of a religious sort."[12]

The constitution or makeup of the jail and prison population in the United States, is comprised of individuals who are in conflict with law, the tenets of our social contract, and those ensnared in the pathologies of neglected communities and adversarial judicial

---

10. Raboteau, "Hidden Wholeness," 5.
11. Matt 22:39–40 (NIV).
12. Opderbeck, *Law and Theology*, 17.

A Theology of Justice

systems. In many contexts within the United States, the law and its tentacles; encompassing the whole of the criminal justice system, is a system designed to protect and enforce laws and societal edicts, constructed by those who have historically benefited from so-called *Law and Order*.

Too often, in communities of color and poor communities, the law has been instrumentalized to criminalize behaviors that have been informed through egregious social conditions. "The law as an instrument of oppression constitutes a fundamental challenge to the rule of law. In such instances, the law, losing its dignity, degenerates into a tool that power wielders handle exclusively for their own interests."[13] Further exasperating the problem is that miscarriages of justice are now flouted with impunity. "In any event, the management of public affairs in a given country can be so far away from justice and equity that the concept of the rule of law may become a mockery. Whoever has endured injustice by law for decades, and perhaps even centuries, will not easily praise the rule of law."[14]

African Americans and persons of color are not lawless. *Law and Order* are precepts that must be grounded in justice and fairness. Law must be tethered to principles which value the intrinsic worth of all people. Opderbeck integrates positive law and natural law. "Legitimate positive law participates in the natural law, which participates in God as an aspect of creation. Legitimate positive law restrains evil, mirrors God's purposes for creation, guides Christians and non-Christians alike . . . and embodies the kingdom of God through liberation from oppression."[15]

This book is an ethnographic work chronicling my tenure inside of the Maryland Department of Corrections over a fifteen year period, beginning in 1992 and culminating in 2007, as director of religious services and chaplaincy, and as director of treatment services from 2008 through 2010 at the Adams County Adult Correctional Complex in Gettysburg, Pennsylvania. It is

---

13. Shelton, *Oxford Handbook*, 489.
14. Shelton, *Oxford Handbook*, 490.
15. Opderbeck, *Law and Theology*, 140.

thus written in the first-person narrative, yet at the same time, draws significantly upon the quantitative scholarly research and insights of social contract theorists and other political philosophers and theologians. The ensuing chapters of this book will cite instruments and mechanisms representative of *best practices* of the time period. This includes referencing *good law* and cases of the particular era, as well as mechanisms and instruments such as the *DSM-IV Diagnostic and Statistical Manual of Mental Disorders*, in use from 1994 through 2013. This instrument was superseded by the DSM-V in 2013. This is significant in order to authenticate the use of *best practices* guiding our work and conclusions within this time period.

Where appropriate, I will cite names of individuals and institutions in the narrative, whose cases and legal circumstances appear in media forums; and are public knowledge, appearing in the public domain. In instances requiring adherence to privacy rights only first names are referenced.

There are thirty-eight ethical statements/principles throughout the seven chapters of *A Theology of Justice*. These ethical statements as a whole form a comprehensive corrections ethic informed by the human rights abuses occurring in jails and prisons within the United States, offering evidence-based correctives. This corrections ethic is informed by my twenty years of qualitative research inside four jail and prison institutions, as an administrator of treatment and religious services departments, including the United States Disciplinary Barracks at Leavenworth, United States Penitentiary in Atlanta, Maryland Division of Pretrial Detention and Services, and the Adams County Adult Correctional Complex in Gettysburg, Pennsylvania. It is my hope that this work is foundational toward a corrections ethic, reflective of disciplines possessing extensive research in the development of its ethics—such as business ethics and medical ethics.

As of this writing the United States incarcerates more of its citizens than any other *civilized country* in the world, to use United Nations language. A peer-reviewed report by *Statista* provides alarming numbers. "As of July 2021, the United States had the highest number of incarcerated individuals worldwide, with almost 2.1 million people in prison. The U.S. was followed by China, Brazil, India, and the Russian Federation."[16]

The problems that contribute to debilitating conditions within correctional facilities range from the tension between treatment and custodial care or security, under-qualified individuals serving on jail and prison disciplinary hearing boards/panels, the ethical dilemma of the misuse and abuse of solitary confinement, institutional methods of control involving cell extraction teams and use of restraint chairs, overcrowded jails and prisons, incarcerating and housing the seriously mentally ill, housing juveniles within adult jail and prison populations, the unique problem of housing female inmates, and housing LGBTQ or transgender populations within the general population.

Increasingly, juvenile offenders are processed in the manner of adults, yet without the benefit of adult psychological development, to accommodate or process the trauma experienced while incarcerated. Riya Saha and Jessica Feierman, writing for the *American Bar Association*, in "Strip-Searching Children Is State-Imposed Trauma" chronicle the ordeal.

> A published opinion from the Third Circuit Court of Appeals provides a glimpse into a deeply problematic practice: On a Friday afternoon, 12 year-old J.B. went to the state police barracks with his parents upon request of a police officer following an incident in his neighborhood three weeks prior. At the station, police processed J.B. on a petition charging him and then transported him to a detention center. He went through the intake process at the detention center and was taken to be strip-searched. An officer observed him remove his clothing. J.B. was asked to turn around, drop his pants and underwear, bend over, spread his buttocks, and cough. He remained unclothed for 90 seconds. J.B. spent the weekend in detention. On Monday morning, J.B. appeared for the first time before a judge in juvenile court who determined his detention was unnecessary and released him to his

---

16. Szmigiera, "Countries with the Most Prisoners," para. 1.

Theological Arguments in Conversation

parents. But the harmful invasion of his privacy couldn't be undone, and J.B.'s case is not unique.[17]

The resulting consequences of suicide in jails and prisons, prison rape and violence, the spread of HIV and AIDS in jails and prisons, and the normalizing of generational criminal deviant behavior within underdeveloped or neglected communities-as a pathway to incarceration, are among the problems that inform this book. This research is significant, because it is also concerned with the external conditions within US society, which contribute to criminogenic pathologies including poverty, social location, drug and alcohol addiction and dependence, undiagnosed mental illnesses, dysfunctional familial patterns, underperforming pedagogical institutions, and a criminal justice system struggling with the juxtaposition of rehabilitative and punitive justice.

There are many good and well-intended individuals who work within correctional facilities in jails and prisons around the country. Career correctional personnel often begin their careers with the noblest of intentions. Some are initially idealistic concerning working with incarcerated individuals and being instrumental in their rehabilitation. At the least there are individuals working within correctional settings who have no lofty ideals of changing the world, but are there simply to make an honest living.

Many are unaware of their complicity in the effects of a jail and prison system that have insidious and egregious implications for an entire demographic and, by extension, their communities. Most are not sophisticated or discerning enough to deconstruct the surreptitious debilitating implications for the inmates and their immediate communities in general, nor the obsessive preoccupation of the larger American culture in general relative to incarceration.

Arguably, there are individuals working within the correctional setting who are either corrupted by the culture, or are willing participants in the corrupting of the jail and prison culture. I have witnessed both.

---

17. Saha and Feierman, "Strip-Searching Children," 16.

A Theology of Justice

As a director within the Division of Pretrial Detention and Services in Maryland, between 1992 and 2007, what was then a three thousand detainee correctional facility located in Baltimore, I recall working with a correctional officer who at the time was enjoying a long tenure within the division. It was around the time that tobacco products were being banned from the jails and prisons under the control of the Maryland Department of Corrections.

An unintended result of this ban was the lucrative black market it created within the correctional facility for the sale of tobacco. Cartons of cigarettes are marked up to astronomical prices inside of jails and prisons, thereby creating a strong incentive for correctional officers and civilian workers to be lured into the black market sale of tobacco to inmates. An article written in April 2006 titled "Contraband Floods Maryland Prisons," by Greg Garland of the *Baltimore Sun*, describes the problem: "Tobacco, banned in Maryland prisons since 2001, has become the most smuggled commodity and is a major source for inmate entrepreneurs. A thin, hand-rolled cigarette can sell for $3 to $6. A pound of loose tobacco that costs $100 to get into prison can bring upward of $1,000 once inside, correctional officers say."[18]

Unfortunately, the allure of the black market entrepreneurial opportunity proved to be too lucrative for the correctional officer. After weeks of surveillance, an internal investigation uncovered evidence that the correctional officer was smuggling contraband into the jail for sale to the detainees. Mysteriously, the correctional officer at the center of the undercover investigation was murdered in Baltimore several weeks after the investigation. Rumors that the killing was an assassination were rampant.

As a director at the Maryland Division of Pretrial Detention and Services, I vividly recall being so concerned with the pungent smell of marijuana being smoked inside of the jail, on what was then known as "R" Section for protective custody, that I worried aloud if one could test positive for marijuana being breathed, if chosen for a random drug urinalysis for which I was selected

---

18. Garland, "Contraband Floods Maryland Prisons," 1.

Theological Arguments in Conversation

often. Detainees smoked marijuana with impunity during my fifteen-year tenure at the facility. It became a running joke.

Another problem at the Maryland Division of Pretrial Detention and Services during my tenure was that of fraternization. Rumors were ubiquitous, concerning inmates and correctional officers and staff carrying on sexual and intimate relationships with the inmate population. On one occasion, I recall being invited to attend an event for a staff member, who worked at the Maryland Division of Pretrial Detention and Services, only to learn upon arrival that his fiancé was an ex-offender who had just recently been released from the jail.

Perhaps one of the most egregious abuses of power by a correctional officer during my tenure occurred in September of 2002. Correctional officer Draughon, who was responsible for transporting female detainees housed in the Women's Detention Center to and from court for their court hearings, allegedly coerced a female detainee into engaging in a sexual encounter during her transport. Once officials were alerted to the allegation an investigation was initiated. Draughon was eventually fired and placed on trial after DNA evidence corroborated the allegation by the female detainee.

On May 14, 2005, one of the most blatant atrocities of my tenure occurred in the Central Booking unit of the Maryland Division of Pretrial Detention and Services. Although the circumstances are unclear and there are conflicting accounts of what occurred that day, one thing is very clear. An inmate was murdered at the hands of correctional officers, during what appeared to be either a cell extraction or a cell insertion. A cell extraction is when an inmate is forcibly removed from his or her cell against their will. A cell insertion occurs when an inmate is forcibly placed into his or her cell against their will.

Within the correctional facility, the unofficial report suggested that the correctional officers became enraged when the inmate inappropriately made overtures to a female correctional officer. The resulting beating that occurred was severe enough to take the life of inmate Raymond K. Smoot. The next day I was instructed to visit the family of the inmate, on the behalf of the Maryland

A Theology of Justice

Division of Pretrial Detention and Services, at The Johns Hopkins Hospital in Baltimore City.

I recall seeing the inmate at the hospital while he was still on life support. I was horrified and angered by what I witnessed. Inmate Raymond K. Smoot was unrecognizable as a result of the beating. His face was disfigured in a way that was reminiscent of civil rights era pictures of Emmett Louis Till, who was murdered in Mississippi at the age of fourteen.

Although I was not an immediate witness to the beating of inmate Raymond Smoot, I witnessed excessive aggression by correctional officers at the Maryland Division of Pretrial Detention and Services over a fifteen-year period. Correctional officers, responding to what is known as a *code* or an emergency within the correctional facility, face uncertainty and great danger upon arriving on the scene of an inmate disturbance. It takes a highly trained correctional officer to maintain a level of professionalism and self-control during a highly charged exercise.

Unfortunately, I witnessed too many correctional officers unable to maintain this difficult equilibrium, and engage in excessive force against inmates. On that fateful day in May of 2005 correctional officers crossed the line. An August 20, 2005 news article written by *Baltimore Sun* journalist Gus G. Sentementes described the occurrence. Sentementes writes,

> Three former state correctional officers were arrested yesterday after a Baltimore Grand Jury indicted them on second-degree murder charges in the stomping death of a 51 year-old man jailed at the Central Booking and Intake Center. The death of Raymond K. Smoot in May came during a brutal melee that spurred federal and state investigations and cast a glaring spotlight on troubles at the beleaguered facility, which holds people who have been charged with crimes but not yet tried in court.[19]

The obvious question to the outside observer may be, to what extent are those presently and previously employed by jails and prisons complicit in the egregious conditions of jails and prisons?

---

19. Sentementes, "Officers Indicted in Death," paras. 1–2.

Theological Arguments in Conversation

Although I never participated in the beatings of inmates, or the abuse of inmates physically or mentally, what did I do to ameliorate their circumstances? Not enough! Although I take great pride in my work within treatment, during my seventeen-year tenure with both the Maryland Division of Pretrial Detention and Services and the Adams County Adult Correctional Complex, too often the concern for employment trumped my empathy for inmate suffering. Whatever protest I did make as an employee—and I did make many—it was too little but hopefully not too late as I write this corrections ethic.

Ethic One—Perhaps one of the first rudimentary requirements in a substantive corrections ethic, is that true jail and prison reform must be instigated by persons external to the administration of jails and prisons. It is not possible to be a prison reformer from the inside. The restraints and pressure for self-preservation ultimately will be too enormous to enact the kind of change that qualifies for jail and prison reformation. Those inside the jails and prisons can do well and act humanely; however, far-reaching prison reform must be done by those who are not impacted by the fear of reprisal by jail and prison officials. Jail and prison reform must be done from the outside. This is true not only for jail and prison employees but ex-offenders as well.

One challenge facing jail and prison reformers, and a substantive corrections ethic, is persuasive education of the public, as to what constitutes humane and inhumane treatment of inmates. The humane treatment of inmates is not a subjective individual opinion. The rights of prisoners should be impervious to political changes within culture and society. Certain conditions within jails and prisons have been mandated by law, recognized under United Nations Human Rights, and codified within mechanisms of the Universal Declaration of Human Rights, most notably under General Assembly Resolution 45/111 of December 14, 1990.

These safeguards must be monitored and enforced by outside reformers or watch groups. During my tenure in the correctional setting of which I write, *Rhodes v. Chapman* and *Helling v. McKinney* were considered *good law* and were the standard applied to

A Theology of Justice

correctional facilities. An article written by Erin Sullivan on May 19, 2004, appearing in the *Baltimore City Paper*, amplifies the need for outside agitation concerning the required standards of jail and prison operations. Sullivan writes,

> Conditions are unconstitutional if they amount to unquestioned and serious deprivations of basic human needs or the minimal civilized measures of life's necessities (Rhodes v. Chapman 1981). . . . A remedy for unsafe conditions need not await a tragic event (Helling v. McKinney 1993). Prison authorities may not ignore a condition of confinement that is sure or very likely to cause serious illness and needless suffering the next week or month or year merely because no harm has yet occurred. Things that people take for granted—clean clothing and bedding, decent nutrition, access to necessary medical care, and safety—the plaintiffs in the suit charge, are not consistently provided at the Baltimore City Detention Center, especially for women at the jail who tend to endure even worse conditions than the men.[20]

During my time at the Maryland Division of Pretrial Detention and Services, I would often say that the floors are buffed to a shine so well, that you can see yourself get shanked in the reflection of the buffed floors. Shanks, which are handmade knives, are made and used by inmates for either protection or as weapons for aggression. Stabbings, beatings, hangings, medical emergencies not responded to, wrong medications administered to inmates, and other abuses were commonplace during my tenure from May of 1992 through May of 2007.

One of the last remembrances I have of my tenure at the Maryland Division of Pretrial Detention and Services, and one that haunts me to this day, is a telephone call I placed to the family of an inmate held in the Central Booking unit of our facility. Because our detention center was located in the infamous East Baltimore side of the city, a side of town riddled with drugs, prostitution, and homicide, it was commonplace to make death notifications

20. Sullivan, "Corrections," 7.

Theological Arguments in Conversation

by protocols other than making a professional visit to the home of inmate families.

This method was justified for several reasons. First, many of the inmates were notoriously transient, lacking a fixed address. Second, too many neighborhoods were dangerous and would pose a risk to anyone associated with the correctional facility. For these reasons I placed a call to the mother of an inmate who had just turned eighteen years of age, and therefore placed into the general population of the jail, as opposed to the juvenile section of the institution.

I called the mother on the telephone and informed her that her son had passed away at the jail. It was either jail policy or the policy of my department, that details surrounding the death of an inmate not be furnished at the level of directors or staff. I was well aware at that time that the inmate was found hanged in his cell. I have the memory of the shrieking and agonized screams of the mother to this day. I regret not going to the residence of the mother of the deceased inmate.

There are certain principles which are so foundational to who we are as human beings, that one does not need a policy and procedure manual to instruct one as to what is the proper course of action, or as how to behave toward another human being. The Latin phrase *Mala in Se* informed by *Natural Rights* captures this. It suggests that there are universal principles transcendent of human ingenuity and design, and that are congenital to the human condition, of which most, if not all, human beings have capacity for; a type of *compassio* or *sympatheia* or what is known as *fellow feeling*. There are wrongs which shock the conscience. It is a wrong we know to be wrong intuitively.

For many staff and administrators within the jails and prisons in the United States, it is correctional policies and procedures that ostensibly exonerate them from personal responsibility for unjust practices. It is what Hannah Arendt might refer to as the *banality of evil* for jails and prisons. Often, correctional staff and administrators find their sense of justice and jail and prison policies in conflict.

A Theology of Justice

Ethic Two—An effective corrections ethic must have as its litmus test what John Rawls refers to as *reflective equilibrium*. One is unable to achieve *reflective equilibrium* as an official within the jail or prison. It is not until an official is outside of the system that he or she can reflect accurately upon the policy and procedure mechanisms governing correctional institutions, and give useful feedback in order to inform and reform the aforementioned policy and procedure mechanisms. In *A Theory of Justice* Rawls states the following:

> When a person is presented with an intuitively appealing account of his sense of justice . . . he may well revise his judgments to conform to its principles even though the theory does not fit his existing judgments exactly. He is especially likely to do this if he can find an explanation for the deviations which undermines his confidence in his original judgments and if the conception presented yields a judgment which he finds he can now accept. From the standpoint of moral theory, the best account of a person's sense of justice is not the one which fits his judgments prior to his examining any conception of justice, but rather the one which matches his judgments in reflective equilibrium.[21]

In April of 2008, I arrived in Gettysburg, Pennsylvania, as the director of the treatment department at the Adams County Adult Correctional Complex. During this time, my conceptualization of justice was significantly informed, and served to further shape my paradigm of a corrections ethic.

It was during this period that I witnessed the unnecessary dissolution of families, due to the egregious jail policy and procedure mechanisms pertinent to our female inmate population. I cannot overstate the importance of the maintenance of familial structures, in both the rehabilitative and recidivist aim of a competent corrections ethic. Central to treatment within corrections is the reduction of recidivism and the reintegration of ex-offenders back into society. Criminologists versed in the discipline of

---

21. Rawls, *Theory of Justice*, 42–43.

Theological Arguments in Conversation

treatment recognize the central role of familial structures within rehabilitative models, and therefore this a primary focus of corrections ethics.

The social contract as espoused by the late Harvard political philosopher John Rawls would define the family as a social institution. It is within this social institution that individuals learn how to live within the boundaries of rules and community expectations, that are *simpatico* with larger societal expectations. The assumption here is that the ethos of the family will reflect what society considers normative behavior. In later chapters, we will examine what happens when the values perpetuated within marginalized communities are internalized through familial structures. At times these values are countercultural, and constitute a growing population with criminogenic tendencies that are learned within the family ethos.

Unfortunately, the increasing jail and prison population in the United States reflects many of the communities on the fringe of society, decimated by pathologies emanating from broken families, missing fathers, and the dismissal of marriage as a traditional institution. Therefore, the family as a social institution may serve as an incubator for either well-adjusted individuals or maladjusted persons.

Writing in *Justice for Earthlings*, in an article titled "Equality of Opportunity and the Family," Susan Okin—the renowned feminist political philosopher—describes Rawls's treatment of the family as a social institution. While Okin is at times critical of Rawls, it is clear that the significance of the family in Rawls's conceptualization of justice is front and center in his thought.

> One of Susan Okin's main achievements in political philosophy . . . was to place the institution of the family at the centre of the theory of social justice. And in the case of the modern political philosopher whose work she admired most—John Rawls—she detected and criticized a profound ambivalence in his treatment of the family. Rawls wavered between seeing the family as a key component of the basic structure of society-by virtue of its pervasive effects on the life chances of its members-and

A Theology of Justice

therefore as central to the theory of justice, and viewing it as a private association on which, accordingly, principles of justice were to bear only peripherally.[22]

Ethic Three—A comprehensive corrections ethic should have as a requirement the incorporation of education programming into the goals and measures of inmate treatment plans. Inmate treatment plans outline the strategies and guidelines to be followed by clinicians in treating inmates. Evidenced-based, pedagogically informed curricula that emphasizes skills focusing upon healthy relationships, relative to parenting and other family dynamics, are essential to a corrections ethic.

While at the Adams County Adult Correctional Complex, programs such as Girl Scouts Beyond Bars were routinely denied access to female inmates incarcerated at the complex. Girl Scouts Beyond Bars is a successful prison program that reunites incarcerated female inmates with their daughters during the incarceration period. Children are allowed to visit and spend the day involved in an activity with their mother.

The result is that the emotional bond is strengthened, and when appropriate the mother can continue as a central figure in the life of the child. Programs such as these are often denied ostensibly for security concerns, a catch-all phrase, or the default position of the institution when it has no will or desire to facilitate a program. The reticence of some jail and prison officials toward such programming, is the result of misguided correctional philosophy, and outdated thinking relative to punishment and rehabilitation. An effective corrections ethic must then concern itself with what Rawls refers to as the family social institution.

Arguably, the most egregious neglect of inmates during my tenure as director of treatment at the Adams County Adult Correctional Complex was in relation to inmates presenting with serious mental illnesses. A further discussion of mental illness among the inmate population will take place in subsequent chapters of this book.

22. Miller, *Justice for Earthlings*, 115–16.

Theological Arguments in Conversation

During my tenure at the Adams County Adult Correctional Complex beginning in 2008, the universally referenced instrument used to assess mental health was the DSM-IV, which has now been superseded by the DSM-V. The references throughout this chapter will refer to the DSM-IV instrument to include *Axis I-V*, which are no longer used as a classification in DSM-V.

Universally, therapeutic communities relied upon and made use of an instrument known as the DSM-IV, which was an abbreviation for *Diagnostic and Statistical Manual of Mental Disorders*. A good description is given in the fifth edition of *Contemporary Behavior Therapy* by Michael D. Spiegler and David C. Guevremont. Spiegler and Guevremont write,

> Diagnosis involves classifying clients' problems into discrete categories of disorders. The American Psychiatric Association developed the standard diagnostic categories used today, and they are available in the 1994 publication of the Diagnostic and Statistical Manual of Mental Disorders (4th edition), which is referred to as DSM-IV, and in a minor text revision published in 2000 (DSM-IV-TR). . . . In fact, most behavior therapists do assign DSM-IV diagnoses. In clinical practice, the major reason for doing so is that official diagnoses are required by clinics, hospitals, schools, and social service agencies before treatment and services can be offered and by health insurance companies before treatment will be paid for. Another potential benefit of diagnosis is that it provides a common language for clinicians to communicate about disorders, and it allows different researchers to assume that they are studying the same basic clinical phenomena.[23]

This instrument is divided into at least five categories, each one referred to as an axis. Axis I: Clinical Disorders, most V-Codes, and conditions that need Clinical attention; Axis II: Personality Disorders and Mental Retardation; Axis III: General Medical

---

23. Spiegler and Guevremont, *Contemporary Behavior Therapy*, 82.

A Theology of Justice

Conditions; Axis IV: Psychosocial and Environmental Problems and Axis V: Global Assessment of Functioning Scale.[24]

The Global Assessment of Functioning is very important as a determinant of how well the patient—inmate in this context—is able to function in his or her environment. The GAF as it is referred to is also valuable because it gives doctors and clinicians, wardens, and jail and prison personnel in this context, insight into how well inmates are able to adhere to jail and prison policies and rules. The DSM-IV-TR describes how the GAF may be used.

> Axis V is for reporting the clinician's judgment of the individual's overall level of functioning. This information is useful in planning treatment and measuring its impact, and in predicting outcome. The reporting of overall functioning on Axis V can be done using the Global Assessment of Functioning (GAF) scale. The GAF Scale may be particularly useful in tracking the clinical progress of individuals in global terms, using a single measure. The GAF Scale is to be related with respect only to psychological, social, and occupational functioning.[25]

More often than not, inmates will present with what is commonly referred to as having a dual diagnosis, or co-occurring disorders. This is when a patient—inmate in this context—suffers from a multiplicity of mental health illnesses, and/or accompanied by drug and alcohol abuse or dependency, or comorbidity. In an article titled "What Is the Difference between Dual Diagnosis vs Co-occurring Disorders?," the two disorders are delineated and defined.

> Co-occurring disorders are very similar to dual diagnosis in that it is usually in reference to two or more health issues occurring at the same time. However, co-occurring disorders is usually in reference to a mental health disorder that developed as a result of substance abuse and addiction to drugs and alcohol. It can also be

---

24. See "DSM-IV Multiaxial System."
25. Bell, "Diagnostic and Statistical Manual of Mental Disorders," 32.

Theological Arguments in Conversation

used to refer to a mental illness that contributes to the development of an addiction.[26]

When I arrived at the Adams County Adult Correctional Complex in Gettysburg, Pennsylvania, I requested that the treatment personnel provide the treatment plans to include the DSM-IV information for the inmate population. The treatment staff were unable to produce such documentation, and were at a complete loss as to what I was requesting.

In frustration and in disbelief I requested a meeting with the warden, seeking insight. I was mortified to learn that the warden of the correctional facility, was unaware of what a treatment plan with DSM-IV information was. This episode began a lengthy and contentious attempt to restructure the entire treatment department.

The first step was to introduce the treatment staff, as well as the warden, to the DSM-IV instrument as well as the basic structure of the treatment plan. The logic being, if the inmate population did not have a proper diagnosis then the correctional officers, as well as the administration, would be unable to discriminate between an inmate being incorrigible as a result of challenging the system, or presenting with a serious mental illness.

The first inmate to be considered for a treatment plan was Robert. I will use only the first name of the inmate due to confidentiality and the professional code of ethics. Robert was selected to have a treatment plan because the jail at the time was unable to control his behavior. Robert was consistently challenging the correctional staff, and was one of the most unpredictably aggressive inmates I had witnessed in my corrections career spanning almost two decades at that time.

On a daily basis, the correctional officers were using what is known in corrections as the SERT Team to deal with Robert. This is the Special Emergency Response Team, and is responsible for making cell extractions or cell insertions, and responding to riots or other inmate disturbances. Whenever a SERT Team is used the

---

26. "What Is The Difference," para. 4.

A Theology of Justice

risk of serious injury or death is increased exponentially. In Maryland we referred to this unit as "The Men in Black."

The SERT would routinely be called to extract Robert from his cell when they needed him to come out, and to insert him into the cell when they needed him to return. Robert would not cooperate on most days. My concern was heightened given that Robert was a man of middle age, and would be highly susceptible to heart attack or death, given the enormous violence which accompanies cell extractions and insertions.

When Robert would resist the commands of the correctional officers, they would become antagonized and take it as a personal affront to their authority and status. Realizing the impasse which existed, I made an appointment with the warden to discuss Robert. The initial response was one of denial that a problem existed, other than the behavior of the inmate. I communicated that perhaps a treatment plan for Robert would give us better insight into his disruptive behavior. The request was given only minimal consideration and went unaddressed for several weeks.

During that time, Robert's disruptive behavior escalated to the point that the warden requested a meeting with me. The warden was now willing to have the inmate placed on a treatment plan, and agreed to an unspecified period of time to evaluate the process. Placing Robert on a treatment plan brought visceral protests, by not only the correctional officers assigned to Robert's unit, but also by the lead mental health clinician provided by our contractual medical provider PrimeCare.

The reasons given by both parties were their assertions that the inmate was feigning mental illness. I recall an email sent out by the mental health clinician to the treatment staff, to respond to Robert as you would any other inmate. I immediately sent out an email that superseded the order regarding inmate Robert. The new order mandated that any punitive action relative to Robert be presented to the director of treatment before any action would be taken. Thus began a contentious conflict that would portend the nature of my career at the facility for the two-year period of my tenure.

Theological Arguments in Conversation

My observations of the inmate over the next several weeks and month to follow consisted of the inmate drinking water from the toilet of his single-man cell. These observations were made without the knowledge of the inmate that he was being observed. Further, Robert would place his hair in small braids and wrap them with some type of paper, with what appeared in texture to be fecal matter. Robert would consistently defecate and smear the substance on his cell window.

One day while particularly agitated, Robert, a self-described former amateur boxer, took his fist and punched and shattered what was thought to be a shatterproof glass in his holding cell door. The inmate was absolutely out of control. A code was called and Robert was restrained and sent to the hole, or what is commonly known as solitary confinement.

Feeling desperate to demonstrate results with Robert and the treatment plan, amidst ridicule from the correctional facility that the treatment plan did not work, I inquired as to the results of the psychological evaluation conducted on the inmate. The results would change the dynamics of how the correctional facility viewed Robert, as well as the nature of treatment planning at the facility. The psychological evaluation, without equivocation, indicated that the inmate suffered from a dual diagnosis, and a low global assessment of functioning (GAF).

Robert was committed to a mental health facility in Pennsylvania for treatment, and returned to the Adams County Adult Correctional Complex thereafter. The diagnosis was instrumental in arguing Robert's case, and helped to make the argument that his sentence should be reduced. Due to Robert's mental illness, he had significantly accrued additional jail time as a result of infractions he had been found guilty of by the jail disciplinary hearing board; comprised of jail personnel often lacking either education credentials, or experience, that would qualify them for such evaluations of inmates.

Inmate Robert received the mental health attention he needed, and was released from the Adams County Adult Correctional Complex. I felt a sense of vindication, but also exasperation, from the resulting acrimony engendered over the treatment plan initiative at the correctional complex. The ensuing resentment between the warden, and the lead clinician, in relationship to me as the director of treatment would prove to be insurmountable. I would leave my position as director of treatment short of two years of service.

Inmate Robert was significant in helping to shape my corrections ethics to the extent that I witnessed human debasement, and experienced extraordinary deficits of human compassion and empathy, by those charged with both securing and treating Robert. Robert demonstrated the degree of subhuman behavior to which human beings can regress. The correctional officers and clinicians demonstrated that in the correctional setting, individuals and institutions are dangerously capable of becoming inhumanely desensitized.

A little-known truth concerning corrections: not only do inmates become institutionalized, but correctional staff and administrators become institutionalized as well. It is a hazard of the profession.

Ethic Four–An effective corrections ethic must have as a central goal an emphasis on understanding the uniqueness of the individual, or even groups of highly difficult inmate populations. A thorough diagnosis, during the intake process, to include classification and treatment planning, of not only the *Presenting Problem* but the origin of their behavioral problems, will give substantive and substantial insight relative to responding to inmate delinquency and malfeasance.

A select group of inmates are incapable of following the regimented policies as outlined in the inmate handbook, which is given to inmates during a process known as intake, due to limited intellect, mental illness, dual diagnosis, or little to no education. In *A Theory of Justice* John Rawls refers to this reality as *natural assets*. Rawls writes,

> Nor does anyone know his fortune in the distribution of natural assets and liabilities, his intelligence, strength, and the like. . . . The existing distribution of income and

wealth, say, is the cumulative effect of prior distributions of natural assets—that is, natural talents and abilities—as these have been developed or left unrealized, and their use favored or disfavored over time by social circumstances and such chance contingencies as accident and good fortune.[27]

Ethic Five—Corrections ethics must take into account those lacking the requisite natural assets to function in society, and within the rules and regulations of jails and prisons.

---

27. Rawls, *Theory of Justice*, 11, 62–63.

Chapter 2

JOHN RAWLS AND SOCIAL CONTRACT THEORY CONCEPTS

THIS CHAPTER EXPLORES THE ways in which Rawls's theory may be used to construct a corrections ethic in the context of jail and prison culture for correctional facilities in the United States. It considers the varied and complex challenges faced while attempting the humane treatment of those incarcerated. The tradition of social contract theory espoused in the writings of such political philosophers as John Locke, Thomas Hobbes, Jean-Jacques Rousseau, and more recently amplified in the work of the Harvard political philosopher John Rawls, is explored and interpreted. This chapter creates a context for the creation of a corrections ethic grounded in social contract theory.

Ethic Six—John Rawls posits that the foremost characteristic of a social institution should be the concern of *just* institutions. Institutions such as the correctional facilities which make up jails and prisons in the United States, should incorporate a humane corrections ethic into its culture through jail and prison policy and procedure mechanisms. The social contract theory as espoused by John Rawls in *A Theory of Justice* conceptualizes how a just society and just institutions would function through the introduction of many of its principles.

John Rawls and Social Contract Theory Concepts

Social contract theory as conceptualized by John Rawls, in principle, emphasizes many of the tenets and values of Christian theology justice pedagogy, within the context of political philosophy. Rawls' principles can be used to articulate principles of justice, common to the Judeo-Christian tradition and Western political philosophy in many instances. This is particularly useful as a method for implementing a humane corrections ethic into the policy and procedure mechanisms, and the standard operating procedures mechanisms at the correctional administration level.

Principles of justice are more significant than parochial language related to theology or religion, because the language used in jail and prison facilities within policy and procedure mechanisms, are always inherently nonreligious. Principles of justice are more important than prose or nomenclature. Capturing the values of Jesus's teachings, and the principles of didactic teachings—the essence of Christianity, Judaism, or Islamic theology or religion—when they focus on human rights and dignity, capturing these principles within the essence of corrections ethics, as well as jail and prison policy and procedure mechanisms should be the focus.

Further, the correctional system at present emphasizes custodial containment as opposed to rehabilitative treatment.

Social contract theory, and the prophetic voice of the Hebrew Bible and New Testament writings, justify a corrections ethic reflective of humane treatment. Arguably, the character of a civilization can be judged, based upon how it responds to the disenfranchised and marginalized within its society. The jail and prison population often reflect those in society who represent the severely dislocated groups on the fringe of society. Writing in *Acting Liturgically*, Nicholas Wolterstorff emphasizes this principle. "I take Jesus to be enjoining us to be alert to the obligations placed upon us by the needs of whomever we happen on, and to pay no attention to the fact, that the needy person belongs to a group that is a disdained or disdaining out-group."[1]

The teachings of Christianity, and the tenets of social contract theory, require that adequate resources are allocated toward

---

1. Wolterstorff, *Acting Liturgically*, 250.

the alleviation of suffering, and to the relief of the marginalized and exploited people and groups. Christian literature historically has a prophetic motif which serves as metanarrative throughout both the Hebrew Bible and New Testament writings. Isaiah 61 and Matthew 25 speak to the responsibility of Christians to ameliorate the conditions which marginalize the human dignity and quality of life of people.

As stated, social contract theory as espoused by John Rawls has the capacity to incorporate the tenets of justice-themed Scripture in the vernacular, in the language used in state and government mechanisms and instruments, such as the policy and procedure mechanisms of jail and prison administration. Some of the more well-known Rawlsian concepts extrapolated from John Rawls and used throughout this corrections ethic are *justice* or *the role of justice, principles of justice, original position, veil of ignorance, maximin, the difference principle, reflective equilibrium, primary goods, justice as fairness, natural assets, capacity for moral personality, moral shame,* and *conception of justice.* These aforementioned tenets, as well as less familiar Rawlsian constructs, will be synthesized as well into a coherent corrections ethic in A *Theology of Justice.*

Two of the theological premises undergirding the thesis of shared interest between social contract theory, its tenets, and prophetic literature are:

> The Spirit of the Lord God is upon me, because the Lord has anointed me; He has sent me to bring good news to the oppressed, to bind up the broken-hearted, to proclaim liberty to the captives, and release to the prisoners; to proclaim the year of the Lord's favor, and the day of vengeance of our God; to comfort all who mourn; to provide for those who mourn in Zion; to give them a garland instead of ashes, the oil of gladness instead of mourning, the mantle of praise instead of a faint spirit. (Isa 61:1–3 NRSV)
> Then the king will say to those at his right hand, Come, you that are blessed by my father, inherit the kingdom prepared for you from the foundation of the world for I

John Rawls and Social Contract Theory Concepts

> was hungry and you gave me food, I was thirsty and you gave me something to drink, I was a stranger and you welcomed me, I was naked and you gave me clothing. I was sick and you took care of me, I was in prison and you visited me. (Matt 25:34–36 NRSV)

The theme or understanding of justice is broad and is understood through the prism of the particular ideological, theological, philosophical, political, and sociological location or perspective of the individual or society. There exist competing concepts of justice, and there is a broad ideological expanse which defines justice in very different ways. Demonstrative of this tension is the very different concepts of justice in the writings of John Rawls in *A Theory of Justice*, juxtaposed with Robert Nozick in *Anarchy, State, and Utopia*. Both make compelling arguments for what justice is, or is not.

John Rawls readily points out differing ideological affirmations of justice. Rawls states in *A Theory of Justice* the following,

> One may think of a public conception of justice as constituting the fundamental charter of a well-ordered human association. Existing societies are of course seldom well-ordered in this sense, for what is just and unjust is usually in dispute. Men disagree about which principles should define the basic terms of their association. Yet we may still say, despite this disagreement, that they each have a conception of justice. That is, they understand the need for, and they are prepared to affirm, a characteristic set of principles for assigning basic rights and duties and for determining what they take to be the proper distribution of the benefits and burdens of social cooperation.[2]

The decisive factor of what justice is may best be understood in the contemplation of how one understands the value and worth of the individual, and society's role in the protection or the restoration of individuals who have been devalued either through systems that marginalize, or by self-destructive behaviors. Thomas Paine, known for his book written in 1791, *Rights of Man*, famously

---

2. Rawls, *Theory of Justice*, 5.

wrote: "A Declaration of Rights is . . . by reciprocity, a Declaration of Duties also. Whatever is my right as a man is also the right of another; and it becomes my duty to guarantee as well as to possess."[3]

Again, I have selected John Rawls and social contract theory as a methodology for creating a corrections ethic, due to the parallel metanarrative that exists between prophetic Judeo-Christian writings relative to justice, and philosophical writings such as the *Second Treatise on Government* by John Locke. Rawls describes how justice can best be achieved in a hypothetical environment that has as its goal the rearranging of people and societies in an order that situates them fairly and justly without an advantage by any group.

Building on his idea of *justice as fairness* Rawls makes use of the social contract theory in the tradition of John Locke. Writing in *Second Treatise on Government,* Locke asserts an optimistic view of humanity, and its potential for collective good, by describing humanity's state of nature not as in a state of chaos, as other social contract theorists describe—most notably Thomas Hobbes, to be discussed in later chapters. Locke describes humanity as possessing certain liberties and rights as inherent, or as *natural rights*, possessed by all by virtue of their existence as a human being. Much of the American Bill of Rights extrapolates from John Locke's ideas.

Ethic Seven—An attainable corrections ethic must be grounded in realistic and achievable goals, empirical and measurable, which not only critique the present state of conditions within jails and prisons, but offer measurable and implementable alternatives.

As such, this corrections ethic is written in the tradition of jail and prison reform as opposed to jail and prison abolishment ideation. Prison reform affirms the need for transformation in jails and prisons, but does not go so far as to suggest the total abolishment of the institution of jails and prisons.

Prison abolitionists such as the noted revolutionary Angela Davis (who has done significant work in calling attention to the

---

3. Shelton, *Oxford Handbook*, 189.

John Rawls and Social Contract Theory Concepts

human rights violations perpetrated by jails and prisons) call for the replacement of such institutions; however, abolitionists do not offer a practical alternative at present for dealing with those in society that pose a threat to the general population. This is very much in the vein of the *defund the police* movement as understood in the popular sense, though not in the criminological theory sense, of which oversight mechanisms could be implemented to allocate funding to police departments, based upon the performance of police departments over decades. When done with empirical methods and best practices *defund the police* could be implemented. However, not with anecdotal and impassioned emotions informing the discussion.

The call for the abandonment of jails and prisons in total is utopian and theoretical. *A Theology of Justice* does, however, present an alternative in the final chapters, informed with a practical replacement to the overuse of jails and prisons.

The paradox is that the need for jails and prisons is a result of an unjust society that has created a dystopia, and the dismantling of the jails and prisons would perpetuate a dystopia. Corrections ethics must be grounded in the jail and prison reform tradition for compelling reasons. There are individuals within our society who either are incapable of adherence to societal rules, or who choose not to live within the agreed-upon structures of society—social contract—for reasons to be discussed in subsequent chapters. In either instance, this demographic represents a segment of society that threatens to encroach upon the rights of other members of society. John Rawls refers to this demographic of society as those lacking the *Capacity for Moral Personality*.

Writing in *A Theory of Justice* Rawls makes the following observation.

> We see, then, that the capacity for moral personality is a sufficient condition for being entitled to justice. Nothing beyond the essential minimum is required . . . . When someone lacks the requisite potentiality either from birth or accident, this is regarded as a defect or deprivation. There is no race or recognized group of human beings

that lacks this attribute. Only scattered individuals are without this capacity, or its realization to the minimum degree, and the failure to realize it is the consequence of unjust and impoverished social circumstances, or fortuitous contingencies. Furthermore, while individuals presumably have varying capacities for a sense of justice, this fact is not a reason for depriving those with a lesser capacity of the full protection of justice.[4]

Ethic Eight—Therefore, a realistic corrections ethic must take into consideration those *scattered individuals* in society and create contingencies for their control.

In 1990, at The United States Disciplinary Barracks located at Fort Leavenworth, Kansas, I encountered what would be the first of many encounters with *scattered individuals* who lack the requisite capacity for moral personality. I was assigned as part of a rotating schedule with other army officers to meet with inmates on death row at that time. My initial experience with one death row inmate in particular, who would later have his sentence commuted to life without parole as I recall, was less than spectacular. He was a likable and disarming character. Over the month in which I was assigned, I had many occasions and intimate conversations with him, and others in the general population as well.

Later, upon review of his personnel file, I discovered exactly why he was incarcerated at the disciplinary barracks. Prior to his conviction, this soldier had been assigned to Fort Bragg in North Carolina. During his assignment he raped and nearly decapitated another soldier. An essential characteristic of inmates such as this one is their ability to cause others to relax their defense mechanisms and to gain their trust. This is their weapon of choice.

I am the author of a corrections ethic that calls for the reformation of jails and prisons, and demands justice. I am also a pragmatist in the tradition of jail and prison reform, not abolishment. There needs to be a place for the humane treatment and confinement of individuals—*scattered individuals*—such as the

---

4. Rawls, *Theory of Justice*, 442–43.

John Rawls and Social Contract Theory Concepts

ones I encountered at the Fort Leavenworth Detention Barracks in 1990.

Fort Leavenworth would serve as the introduction to my career in corrections that would span twenty years. These twenty years serve as the basis for my conceptualization of a corrections ethic which mandates and incorporates justice. During my tenure I served in the following capacities, and developed my corrections ethics through my lived experiences with the inmate population, as well as my scholarly formation of theology, ethics, and criminal justice; temporary duty assignment (TDY—a military term) at Fort Leavenworth Detention Barracks; internship at the Atlanta Federal Penitentiary; Maryland Division of Pretrial Detention and Services as a director within Programs and Services-Religious Services for fifteen years; and Adams County Adult Correctional Complex in Pennsylvania, as director of treatment for two years.

Chapter 3

A History of Corrections in the United States

A DISCUSSION OF ETHICS is often conceptualized in terms of individuals, and the conduct of individuals in relationship with one another. However, institutions have a responsibility to possess good moral character, and a specified code of ethical behavior as well. Individual morality and ethical behavior are easily identifiable through the acts or conduct of the actor. Institutions, or institutional conduct, and ethical behavior at times, are more difficult to decipher due to their complexities and evasive locus of accountability.

Specific to the concern of jails and prisons is the inherent tension or flaw in the constitutional makeup of the relationship between inmates and those positioned to maintain the custodial care of inmates. By the nature of corrections and perhaps necessity, the penal system relative to the balance of power is skewed to empower custodians and to disempower the inmate population. This arrangement inherently invites the abuse of power.

Because of the need to control jail and prison populations, this inequity in the balance of power is arguably a necessary evil. Theologian Reinhold Niebuhr, though speaking in a different context, nonetheless captures the reality of abuses of power when

A History of Corrections in the United States

there is an uneven distribution of power. Writing in *Six Theories of Justice: Perspectives from Philosophical and Theological Ethics*, renowned Christian ethics scholar and UCC theologian and colleague Karen Lebacqz captures Niebuhr's sentiment:

> Justice is achieved only as some kind of decent equilibrium of power is established. Niebuhr is perhaps best known for his constant stress on the balance of power: "Any justice that the world has ever achieved rests upon some balance between the various interests." This, he declares, is a "clear lesson of history." This also means that, for Niebuhr, power yields injustice. Niebuhr speaks frequently of the injustice of power: "It may be taken as axiomatic that great disproportions of power lead to injustice." Justice in social systems, therefore, is not simply a matter of how goods are distributed, but is also a question of the proper ordering and balancing of power. The struggle for justice is a struggle to increase the power of the victims of injustice.[1]

Ethic Nine—Correction ethics must acknowledge both the necessity of disproportionality of power in jails and prisons, as well as the inherent abuses that disproportionality inherently brings.

The remedy for this conundrum is found in what Rawls refers to as the *difference principle* in *A Theory of Justice*. The difference principle recognizes and even affirms the inequity in societal arrangements, and that individuals and groups will always find themselves either on the top or bottom strata of society. The difference principle, however, emphasizes that those in positions of power in society are justified in enjoying their standing if in fact *their good fortune* is to the benefit of the larger society as a whole.

Ethic Ten—An effective corrections ethic then must justify the power distribution in jails and prisons as a means to empower inmates through rehabilitative programming and treatment, during their incarceration, as a means to reduce recidivism and facilitate reentry into society.

---

1. Lebacqz, *Six Theories of Justice*, 88–89.

A Theology of Justice

This can be achieved by making educative curricula accessible to the entire inmate population, or through incentivizing inmate participation through reduced sentences, reduction in security levels from maximum to medium to minimum, or increased visitation rights, for example. Writing in *A Theory of Justice* Rawls describes the use of the *difference principle*. "Those who have been favored by nature, whoever they are, may gain from their good fortune only on terms that improve the situation of those who have lost out. The naturally advantaged are not to gain merely because they are more gifted, but only to cover the costs of training and education and for using their endowments in ways that help the less fortunate as well."[2]

Writing in *A Theory of Justice*, John Rawls defines institutions as a public system of rules. Also, Rawls defines how these institutions realize equality in what he refers to as the *Basis of Equality*.

> Now by an institution I shall understand a public system of rules which defines offices and positions with their rights and duties, powers and immunities, and the like.... The first is to the administration of institutions as public systems of rules. In this case equality is essentially justice as regularity. It implies the impartial application and consistent interpretation of rules according to such precepts as to treat similar cases similarly (as defined by statues and precedents) and the like.... The second and much more difficult application of equality is to the substantive structure of institutions. Here the meaning of equality is specified by the principles of justice which require that equal basic rights be assigned to all persons.[3]

Jails and prisons as institutions are challenged in the impartial application and consistent interpretation of rules at several levels. Equality as justice then is negated in the demographics or census of jails and prisons in the United States. The present state of jails and prisons demographically reflect a disproportionate

---

2. Rawls, *Theory of Justice*, 87.
3. Rawls, *Theory of Justice*, 47, 441–42.

representation of the poor, undereducated, persons of color, juveniles, and increasingly, the female population.

Also, a little-known fact about jails and prisons is that once incarcerated it is possible and is often an occurrence that inmates are subjected to disciplinary boards whereby their sentences can be lengthened. Jail and prison disciplinary boards are too often biased by punitive correctional staff, and underrepresented by treatment staff. The unqualified personnel who participate in the jail and prison disciplinary boards do not achieve equality as justice in their lack of expertise in adjudicatory matters, nor in their representation of the correctional institution as an arbiter of fairness, justice, and parity.

The enormity of the jail and prison network in the United States increasingly makes the locus of ethical and moral accountability evasive and opaque. Further compounding this problem is the clandestine nature of jails and prisons as an institution. Jail and prison officials are able to act with impunity, due to the fact that institutions incarcerate those who lack noteworthiness and are perceived by the public as disposable, representative of those in the margins.

Also, jails and prisons have been able to take advantage of the inconclusive philosophy of corrections, relative to punishment and or rehabilitation. Often the public perception of jails and prisons is, with the exception of the most egregious violation of inmate human rights, that inmates deserve any punishment they receive while incarcerated. This public opinion empowers and emboldens correctional officials to act unjustly and unethically with little concern for reprisal.

In the case of jails and prisons, the locus of ethics and moral accountability is difficult to identify due to the stealth nature of the institution that is corrections. Unless the jail or prison is located in an urban area such as the Maryland Division of Pretrial Detention and Services, the isolation of many correctional facilities creates an environment of clandestineness. And unless one is a member of a watch group such as the Pennsylvania Prison Society, or has a relative incarcerated, there is no occasion for the public to venture into the jails and prisons of the United States.

In order to gain some perspective let us turn our attention to the history of jails and prisons in the United States. In the United States, jails are used primarily to incarcerate individuals accused of a crime and are awaiting adjudication. In most instances, jails house detainees for shorter periods of time than do prisons. A misconception is that jails house less dangerous offenders. The reality, however, is that persons accused of the most heinous crimes await trial and sentencing in jails around the country. My encounters with murderers and rapists were at jails in Maryland and Pennsylvania.

Prisons are where offenders serve their sentences once they have been adjudicated by the courts. Inmates serving time in prison are normally housed there for more extensive periods of time. *Alternatives To Prison* by Craig Russell provides a basic definition for jails and prisons.

> Usually, when people are first arrested, they are put in jail. A jail is generally a small facility operated by the local county, city, or town. Unless they can afford bail or are released on just their promise that they will appear for all hearings, people are held in jail until their trials. Jails also hold people convicted of minor crimes. People convicted of major crimes are sent to prisons, which are usually much larger than jails. Most prisons are run by either a state government or by the federal government. Some prisons, however, are run by a business.[4]

The description given by Russell can be used as a good generalization; however, the realities of the contemporary state of incarceration, and of jails and prisons, is that they can produce jails such as Rikers Island in New York which houses approximately fifteen thousand detainees.

Many students of history are well familiar with the landmark work titled *Democracy in America* by Alexis de Tocqueville as a scholarly work of monumental influence. In this classic work de

---

4. Russell, *Alternatives to Prison*, 15.

A History of Corrections in the United States

Tocqueville renders an analysis of the political, social, and institutional structures within America. However, few observers are aware of the occasion of Alexis de Tocqueville's journey to America from France. In an introduction written by Joseph Epstein in *Democracy in America*, Epstein outlines the trip by Gustave de Beaumont and Alexis de Tocqueville to America:

> COUNT (Charles) ALEXIS (Henri Maurice Clerel) DE TOCQUEVILLE was born in Paris on July 29, 1805, to an aristocratic family. During the French Revolution, his parents had been jailed and his grandfather guillotined. His father was restored to his rank and possessions after the reign of Napoleon, and the young de Tocqueville was given a judicial post in the court of Versailles. Despite the excesses of the French quest for equality, he was passionately interested in democratic government. At twenty-six, he used his position as a magistrate to travel to America to study, he said, the prison system. For nine months in 1831 and 1832, he and a friend, Gustave de Beaumont, visited American prisons, conducted interviews, observed the country and its inhabitants, and collected books and documents.[5]

By the time de Tocqueville arrived in America in 1831 the practice of incarcerating individuals had begun in earnest. For approximately fifty-eight years since 1773 the Newgate Prison in Simsbury, Connecticut, had functioned as one of the first verifiable holding cells in America. Originally a mine for copper and silver, the jail was located underground and proved to be a harsh environment for inmates located there. The Simsbury Historical Society describes the origins and conditions at the Newgate Prison. "In May 1773, the Connecticut General Assembly began looking at using the less than financially successful mine to house prisoners in an atmosphere where escape would be impossible ... an underground room 15 by 12 feet.... The name of the new colonial prison eventually became New Gate (the preferred spelling at that time)."[6]

---

5. Tocqueville, *Democracy in America*, xix.
6. Simsbury Historical Society, "Newgate Prison," paras. 3–4.

A Theology of Justice

Newgate prison became infamous for its inhumane conditions. It housed both American prisoners, and eventually British nationals. "New Gate became notorious in England for the underground conditions of dampness, vermin, insects and darkness."[7]

Newgate prison was one of the first institutions to make use of inmate labor for profit in the fledgling colonies, with its use of what has come to be known as the treadmill, tread wheel or the stepping mill. This device made use of inmate generated power to serve as a type of human generator. The earliest use of this device was said to be a mechanism for prisoner reform or rehabilitation. While the intent of the tread wheel may have arguably been for the reform of prisoners, the burgeoning abuse of prison labor for profit is easily identifiable.

Again, the Simsbury Historical Society describes the use of the treadmill at Newgate prison. "In 1824 a 'stepping mill' or treadmill was introduced which allowed those with no skills or serving short sentences a way to labor. The male prisoners would spend 10 minutes walking while holding on to an overhead bar then 5 minutes resting. Approximately 20 men at a time were on the mill. The power it produced was used to grind grain or corn and run various machines."[8]

Although the account of the Simsbury Historical Society relative to the treadmill seems innocuous, other sources describe a more malevolent use of the mechanism. Historically, the treadmill was used to torture slaves through exhaustion, and would result in limbs being caught in the wheel and broken or maimed extremities.

In 1773 and 1790, in the city of Philadelphia, Pennsylvania, the first attempt at jail and prison construction, both literally in physical design and as a methodology in matters of early penology, was realized in the Walnut Street Jail. The Walnut Street Jail is significant in the study of jails and prisons in the United States for many reasons, the first of which is due to its identification as the first penitentiary in the United States. It is from the Walnut Street

---

7. Simsbury Historical Society, "Newgate Prison," para. 4.
8. Simsbury Historical Society, "Newgate Prison," para. 6.

A History of Corrections in the United States

Jail that a new philosophy of housing inmates was born, and this system came to be known as the Pennsylvania System.

The Pennsylvania System was influenced significantly by the Quakers of Pennsylvania, in an effort to achieve a more humane way of housing inmates and facilitating inmate reflection upon their crimes. The word "penitentiary" is reflective of penitence, and was the impetus for what was at that time a new way of thinking about jails and prisons. In order to achieve penitence, the physical structure of the prison was made to isolate the inmates from one another, and to allow them to reflect upon their misdeeds while in isolation or solitary confinement for most of their sentence.

During the developmental stages of penology, there was not a great deal known about the adverse effects of isolation for extended periods of time on persons incarcerated. Armed with good intentions nonetheless, the Quakers designed the blueprint for the philosophy of incarcerating inmates, the likes of which would serve as the model for prisons for years to come. *Prison Reform* by Joel GAzis-Sax concerning origin of prisons, excerpted from *The Handbook of Correctional Institution Design and Construction*, United States Bureau of Prisons, describes the Walnut Street Jail:

> What has been called "the first American penitentiary, if not the first one in the world," was established in Philadelphia, in 1790, in the Walnut Street Jail, a building formerly operated as a city jail, pursuant to the law of 1790, introduced in permanent fashion the structural pattern of outside cells, with a central corridor, the chief architectural feature of the Pennsylvania system of prison construction. Here, for the first time in penological history, the use of imprisonment through solitary confinement as the usual method of combating crime, was permanently established. The basic principles of the new system, so it appears from contemporary accounts, were the effort to reform those in prison, and to segregate them according to age, sex, and the type of the offenses charged against them.[9]

---

9. US Bureau of Prisons, *Correctional Institution Design*, para. 1.

A Theology of Justice

Eventually, the Pennsylvania System would be deemed as inhumane, due to its austerity relative to housing inmates in isolation and disallowing contact with the outside world. A revolutionary contribution of the Pennsylvania System to penology, however, was its classification of prisoners by gender, age, and type of crime. This classification system curtailed to some extent the ubiquitous practice by predatory inmates of victimization of vulnerable inmates.

The next significant movement in the formation of the jail and prison system was the advent of the Auburn Prison, which would give rise to what came to be known as the Auburn System. Auburn Prison is dated by some historians as early as 1816 and others as 1821. The significance of Auburn Prison is that it introduced for the first time the concept of single-cell construction for housing inmates. The Auburn Prison, however, initiated a new era in the philosophy of jails and prisons. It was at Auburn Prison in New York that inmates were subjected to the concept of rehabilitation through hard labor.

Inmates were forced to labor ten hours per day for purported purposes of rehabilitation through the virtue of hard work. The labor the inmates provided was also a source of revenue and called into question the veracity of the rehabilitative motive. The Auburn Prison introduced the now-infamous striped prison uniform, and the inmate marching style referred to as walking in lockstep. Auburn Prison was one of the visits on the itinerary of Alexis de Tocqueville, documented on July 9, 1831.

Auburn Prison has the dubious distinction of conducting the first execution by electric chair in the world. On August 6, 1890, William Kemmler was executed for the murder of Tillie Zeigler, with whom he shared a romantic relationship. The execution is reported to have been botched on the first attempt, but grotesquely successful on an immediate second attempt as reported by the newspapers of the day. In an article titled "New York State Archives: Where History Goes On Record", a succinct description of the Auburn Prison is rendered.

A History of Corrections in the United States

Auburn is the oldest existing State correctional facility. It was built to relieve overcrowding at Newgate Prison in New York City and received its first inmates in 1817. The 'Auburn System' included separate confinement of inmates, congregate work during the day, enforced silence, lockstep walking, striped uniforms, and the use of the lash as punishment. It was the first institution to use separate cells for inmates. There was great interest in this new system throughout the penal community, and Auburn influenced the subsequent construction of many similar prisons in other states. Many of the harsher elements in the Auburn system eventually were phased out by the end of the 19th century.[10]

The new technology of that era would later inform the use of capital punishment as a form of terrorism, within the Black community over a century later. The youngest person executed in the United States was George Stinney Jr., in South Carolina. Stinney was a fourteen-year-old black boy who was electrocuted in 1944. Of course, he was accused of violating a white girl—two in his case. In 2014 George's case was vacated.

The Auburn system of exporting and exploiting inmate labor for profit would portend jail and prison models centuries later.

In 1829 the Eastern State Penitentiary was established in Philadelphia, Pennsylvania. This prison marked a return to the concept of prisoner isolation and penitence through segregation. The Eastern State Penitentiary used the practice of hooding inmates in an effort to prevent them from having eye contact with other inmates during the time they were outside their cell, and in the inner parts of the institution. At the time of its construction and in the years to follow, Eastern State Penitentiary was considered an architectural model, and was the embodiment of the human ingenuity and ambition which seemed to capture the zeitgeist following the American Revolution. Also, Eastern State Penitentiary was understood at the time to be an example of enlightenment, pertinent to prison reformation and penology.

10. "Guide to Records of the Department," 15.

A Theology of Justice

The continued practice of segregating inmates according to gender, and type of crime, continued as a staple of the Pennsylvania System. America, through Eastern State Penitentiary, became a destination for those interested in jail and prison construction and administration from around the world. Eastern State Penitentiary became the model of prison architecture, both in America and in many countries around the world. The fortress-like façade became synonymous with the image in people's minds, as to what prisons looked like for over a century and a half.

Over time, however, the Eastern State Penitentiary would come under increasing criticism, as advancements were made in the understanding of human behavior, and the humane treatment of prisoners. An article written by Chai Woodham for the Smithsonian accurately describes the events.

> Construction of Eastern State Penitentiary began on a cherry orchard outside of Philadelphia in 1822. The chosen design, created by British born architect John Haviland, was unlike any seen before: seven wings of individual cell blocks radiating from a central hub. The penitentiary opened in 1829, seven years before completion, but the institution proved to be a technological marvel. With central heating, flush toilets, and shower baths in each private cell, the penitentiary boasted luxuries that not even President Andrew Jackson could enjoy at the White House. . . .
>
> More than 300 prisons throughout Europe, South America, Russia, China and Japan would be based on the Eastern State Penitentiary model. But some were not so convinced of the method. Charles Dickens, after his visit in 1842, wrote critically: "I am persuaded that those who designed this system . . . do not know what it is they are doing . . . I hold the slow and daily tampering with the mysteries of the brain to be immeasurably worse than any torture of the body."[11]

By the first decade of the twentieth century, the Pennsylvania System with its harsh style of incarceration would be phased out.

11. Woodham, "Eastern State Penitentiary," para. 8.

A History of Corrections in the United States

The demise of the Pennsylvania System, experienced through the Eastern State Penitentiary, recalls John Rawls and his first virtue of social institutions once again. "Justice is the first virtue of social institutions, as truth is of systems of thought. A theory however elegant and economical must be rejected or revised if it is untrue; likewise laws and institutions no matter how efficient and well-arranged must be reformed and abolished if they are unjust."[12] Eastern State Penitentiary was a model in efficiency; however, it failed to achieve justice in the humane treatment of the inmate population.

The jail and prison movement embodied in the Pennsylvania System and Auburn System would in 1876 be overshadowed by a new movement on the horizon, which would serve as a precursor to contemporary jail and prison rehabilitation efforts. This movement would be initiated through the Elmira Reformatory in Elmira, New York. This model would institute for the first time treatment instruments in an attempt to scientifically diagnose inmates, and would create treatment modalities and methodologies as part of their prison reform regimen, with the advances in penology known at that time.

In an article appearing in New York States Department of Correctional Services, titled "History of Elmira," the following description is provided:

> When New York's Elmira Reformatory opened in 1876, it rejected 19th century penology's holy trinity of silence, obedience and labor. Elmira's goal would be reform of the convict, and its methods would be psychological rather than physical. Instead of coercing with the lash, Elmira would encourage with rewards. Mass regimentation would yield to classification and individualized treatment. Instead of fixed sentences to fit the crime, the indeterminate sentence would be adjustable to fit the criminal. Rather than outright release after the offender "paid his debt to society," the new parole procedure would assure he did not begin running up a new tab.[13]

12. Rawls, *Theory of Justice*, 3.
13. "Elmira," para. 1.

Throughout the very early developmental stages of jails and prisons in the United States, there have been persons concerned with the inhumane conditions, and abuse of inmates incarcerated in institutions. In 1787, a group called the Philadelphia Society for Alleviating the Miseries of Public Prisons met in the home of Benjamin Franklin in order to discuss abhorrent jail and prison conditions.

This group would evolve into what is now known as the Pennsylvania Prison Society. In 1913, Thomas Mott Osborne, while serving as the chairman of a prison reform organization, posed as an inmate in the Auburn Prison in order to ascertain what life was like from the inside. An article titled "Thomas Mott Osborne American Penologist," appearing in *Britannica*, gives an account of Osborne inside the prison.

> In 1913 he became chairman of the New York State Commission on Prison Reform, a post that inspired him to spend a week in Auburn Prison as 'Tom Brown" to learn firsthand. Convinced thereby that it is liberty alone that fits men for liberty, he founded a Mutual Welfare League of the Auburn prisoners, which assumed such responsibilities as forming committees to judge violators of prison rules and to plan entertainment events.[14]

WHO PROFITS?

The final section of this chapter addresses the prison privatization or for-profit dilemma of jails and prisons in the United States and even internationally. Our focus will be on the convict lease system, Parchman Farm, Corrections Corporation of America (CoreCivic), GEO Group (formerly Wackenhut Corrections), and Maryland State Use Industries (Maryland Correctional Enterprises).

Let me begin with an ethical repudiation of the prison privatization, for-profit, prison industrial complex. *Ethic Eleven*—An

---

14. "Thomas Mott Osborne American Penologist," para. 2.

effective corrections ethic must affirm that private, for-profit jails and prisons make their profit on the incarceration of men, women, and children. If their numbers are increased, and the inmate population rises, then private and for-profit jails and prisons secure their profitability. When prison numbers are decreased, it is a threat to the viability and sustainability of the private, for-profit, jail and prison economic model. Treatment, and rehabilitative programming, are designed to decrease recidivism and reintegrate the offender back into mainstream society. The attrition of offenders exiting the system of incarceration diminishes the profits of private, for-profit, jails and prisons.

In an article titled "Private Prisons Are a Failed Experiment," in the *ABA Journal*, Matt Reynolds writes on Resolution 507, stating that "The industry lobbies to impose stricter laws and penalties and opposes sentencing reforms. . . . 'Today, private prison corporations are driven by perverse and immoral incentives whereby an increase in crime and an increase in the number of human beings placed into America's prisons is good business news for that industry.'"[15]

Therefore, rehabilitation and treatment are not in the interest of these institutions from a profit standpoint, nor in the best interest of the long term business model.

As early as the 1990s and 2000s, Corrections Corporation of America (which is now CoreCivic) had significant influence in the for-profit jail and prison industry. An article written for CorpWatch, a research group concerned with human rights and corporate impropriety, written by Ken Silverstein in *Prison Legal News* and titled "US: America's Private Gulag," documented the following conflict of interest.

> To be profitable, private prison firms must ensure that prisons are not only built but also filled. Industry experts say a 90–95 per cent capacity rate is needed to guarantee the hefty rates of return needed to lure investors. Prudential Securities issued a wildly bullish report on CCA a few years ago but cautioned, "It takes time to bring

15. Reynolds, "Immoral Incentives," paras. 10–11.

inmate population levels up to where they cover costs. Low occupancy is a drag on profits." Still, said the report, company earnings would be strong if CCA succeeded in ramp(ing) up population levels in its new facilities at an acceptable rate . . .

Private prison companies have also begun to push, even if discreetly, for the type of get-tough policies needed to ensure their continued growth. All the major firms in the field have hired big-time lobbyists. When it was seeking a contract to run a halfway house in New York City, Esmor hired a onetime aide to State Representative Edolphus Towns to lobby on its behalf. The aide succeeded in winning the contract and also the vote of his former boss, who had been an opponent of the project. In 1995, Wachenhut Chairman Tim Cole testified before the Senate Judiciary Committee to urge support for amendments to the Violent Crime Control Act—which subsequently passed—that authorized the expenditure of $10 billion to construct and repair state prisons.[16]

The concept of for-profit and privatization of jails and prisons is not new, however—it has its origins in what is known as the convict lease system. It is generally agreed that the convict lease system began in the south as a means for uncompensated labor, to replace the vacated labor force lost through the abolishment of the formal institution of slavery.

During the formative years of the convict lease system, the growth of jail and prison populations-paralleled the prominence and pervasiveness of the system in many Southern states. In partnership with the University of Georgia, an article for *The New Georgia Encyclopedia* titled "Convict Lease System," the aforementioned correlation is corroborated: "The South relied heavily on slave labor for farming and jobs that required hard labor. But with emancipation and the passage of the Thirteenth Amendment, slavery as an institution and a form of labor became

---

16. Silverstein, "US: America's Private Gulag," paras. 13, 15.

illegal.... Georgians saw the prisoners at the state's penitentiary in Milledgeville as the solution to their problems."[17]

It became clear to entrepreneurs that jail and prison populations provided a significant source of revenue for both the business community, state government, and the institution of jails and prisons. Because of the legacy of the convict lease system, the present-day State Use Industries (rebranded as Maryland Correctional Enterprises) serves as an egregious reminder of the abuses perpetuated by the convict lease system, upon inmates in general, and African American and inmates of color in particular. The fact that inmates working in the State Use Industries (now Maryland Correctional Enterprises) may not suffer the physical torture that accompanied the convict lease system, does not mitigate the horrific historical connection between the two systems. Unfortunately, administrators in the State Use Industries (Maryland Correctional Enterprises) either do not understand their complicity in the continuation of the Convict Lease System, or do not value the human rights of inmates under their supervision.

University of Nevada at Las Vegas criminal justice professor Randall G. Sheldon, writing for *The Black Commentator* in an article titled "Slavery in the Third Millennium Part II—Prisons and Convict Leasing Help Perpetuate Slavery," makes the following observation.

> Convict leasing involved leasing out prisoners to private companies that paid the state a certain fee. The convicts worked for the companies during the day (convicts were usually not paid) outside the prison and returned to their cells at night. Criminologist Thorsten Sellin, in his book *Slavery and the Penal System*, says that the sole aim of convict leasing "was financial profit to the lessees who exploited the labor of the prisoners to the fullest, and to the government which sold the convicts to the lessees." One example was a lease system in Alabama. Sellin explains it as follows:
>> "In 1866, the governor of Alabama leased the penitentiary to the contractor who was charged

---

17. Todd, "Convict Lease System," paras. 1–2.

A Theology of Justice

> the sum of five dollars and given a loan. The legislature granted him permission to work the prisoners outside the walls; they were soon found in the Ironton and New Castle mines."[18]

In our contemporary culture, African American youth can be witnessed romanticizing the images of incarceration as a rite of passage, signifying street credibility and commissioning for participation and leadership in the illegal drug trade and gang affiliation. The insidious systemic pathology of incarceration, easily identifiable in recent African American communities, is traceable to the convict lease system, and other systemic entrepreneurial institutions of servitude vis-à-vis the privatization of probation for-profit industry, that have as their sole purpose mass incarceration for profit.

My grandfather was born ca. 1907 in the state of Georgia. Much of what I know about my grandfather, family members of that era, and their associates involves their work on the railroad. I recall many family discussions reminiscent of the harsh realities of work on the railroad. One of the industries of the convict lease system in the south was the railroad. I theorize that the die was cast in solidifying a caste system within the African American community, via the transition from negro prison labor vis-à-vis the convict lease system, to negros as cheap laborers on the railroad and in other areas of manual labor; in the conceptualization by American culture concerning the social location of African Americans today.

In an article titled "The African-American Railroad Experience," written by Maureen Cavanaugh and Pat Finn, the relationship is examined. "The image of the African-American railroad worker is a staple in the cultural history of America.... The porter became a recognizable character in American art and music and, in the early days of Hollywood.... But the link between African-Americans and the growth of American railroads is much

---

18. Sheldon, "Slavery in the Third Millennium," paras. 6–7.

A History of Corrections in the United States

deeper.... The entire southern railroad network that was built during the slavery era was built almost exclusively by slaves."[19]

Thus, there exists a continuum from the institution of slavery, to the convict lease system, to the American railroad system and enterprise. The emphasis here is that there has intentionally, consistently, and systematically been a framework for the hegemonic social engineering of negroes, coloreds, Blacks, and African Americans in the United States. This framework has included jails and prisons in the context of the convict lease system, and the contemporary prison industrial complex.

Ethic Twelve—An effective corrections ethic must be capable of deconstructing the systematic network of institutions, practices, and perceptions that perpetuate dysfunctional, traumatized, and criminogenic persons and communities.

Vital institutions which often exclude African Americans—including institutions of higher education and other civil society entities—contribute to the school-to-prison pipeline vexation. Immoral practices of institutions to exclude a particular demographic has led to significant jail and prison proliferation. Retired judge Jay Blitzman describes the school to prison pipeline. "The school-to-prison pipeline (STPP) has been described as a series of practices and policies that funnel children and adolescents from public schools into our juvenile and criminal systems.... The STPP reflects a disturbing and retributive narrative that has contributed to the criminalization of childhood adolescence and has disproportionately affected our most vulnerable populations."[20]

Writing in *A Theory of Justice* Rawls specifies that equal basic rights must be afforded all members of society by institutions. "The second and much more difficult application of equality is to the substantive structure of institutions. Here the meaning of equality is specified by the principles of justice which require that equal basic rights be assigned to all persons."[21]

---

19. Cavanaugh, "African-American Railroad Experience," paras. 1, 6.
20. Blitzman, "Shutting Down the School-to-Prison Pipeline," 20.
21. Rawls, *Theory of Justice*, 442.

A Theology of Justice

Easily, Dante Alighieri's depiction of hell captured in his work *The Inferno* could serve as a description of Mississippi's State Prison known as Parchman Farm in the early twentieth century. Parchman Farm continued the practice of utilizing convicts for profit. Certain historians have gone as far as to assert that Parchman Farm was worse than the institutional system of slavery. This is difficult to fathom. A review by Robert M. Goldman of Virginia Union University cites author David M. Oshinsky, writing in *Worse Than Slavery: Parchman Farm and the Ordeal of Jim Crow Justice*, which describes the conditions down on the farm. "During the Cold War years an article of faith that distinguished the "Evil Empire" of Soviet Communism was the latter's Siberian Gulag. . . . According to David M. Oshinsky, the U.S. did indeed have its own gulag, and it went by the name of Mississippi. Parchman Farm was its first circle."[22]

The harsh conditions found at Parchman Farm were inextricable from the insatiable demand of the burgeoning economy of the south. The Mississippi prison would be utilized as a tributary which streamed labor into the development of a type of *quasi* state rebuilding scheme. Goldman continues in his review of David M. Oshinsky. "As it developed in Mississippi, convict leasing successfully replaced racial bondage with a system of racial castes while at the same time fueling the economic development of the late 19th century New South. . . . There was always a ready supply of replacement labor, so incentives against the mistreatment of convict workers were nonexistent."[23]

The brutality that accompanies forced labor is no coincidence but is a necessary psychological breaking of the inmate-slave's spirit. This type of psychological breaking of the inmate has its roots in the psychological subjugation of the slave to the overseer. Writing in *The Social Contract or Principles of Political Right*, translated by G. H. D. Cole, this phenomenon was not lost on social contract

---

22. Goldman, Review of *Worse Than Slavery*, para. 1.
23. Goldman, Review of *Worse Than Slavery*, para. 3.

philosopher Jean-Jacques Rousseau: "Slaves lose everything in their chains, even the desire of escaping them."[24]

Tragically, institutions and revisionist historians have a way of sanitizing and even romanticizing its most heinous episodes in history. The dystopia that was the Mississippi State Prison at Parchman Farm has been overshadowed by pseudo-historians who celebrate the prison songs that were born out of the tortured conditions on the farm.

Alarmingly, the so-called prison songs that originated at Parchman Farm are eerily reminiscent of the slave songs that originated in the institution of slavery. One need only to listen to live recordings from Parchman, and reenactments of the slave songs, to immediately recognize the cadences, modulations, and intonations as indistinguishable one from the other.[25]

Writing in *H-Net Reviews* in the Humanities & Social Sciences, Brent Aucoin makes the following observation in the review of *Down on Parchman Farm: The Great Prison in the Mississippi Delta*, by William Banks Taylor. "Parchman Farm was home to thousands of Mississippi blacks whose musical tastes and talents led them to memorialize their misery and despair in songs . . . [and] has spurred scholarly indictments of the institution as the epitome of southern injustice: racist, oppressive, archaic, exploitative, and ultimately, 'worse than slavery.'"[26]

Jean-Jacques Rousseau provides a bridge to understanding the replication of the abhorrent legacy of black music and song, exploited at Parchman Farm, in today's popular culture of hip-hop music. Again, Rousseau said *Slaves lose everything in their chains, even the desire of escaping from them*. The legacy of jail and prison is unwittingly perpetuated by hip-hop artists, rap artists, and popular culture through the glamorization of incarceration

---

24. Rousseau, *Social Contract or Principles of Political Right*, 2.

25. One online distributor markets the sale of these recordings as follows. "Prison Songs (Historical Recordings From Parchman Farm 1947–48), Vol. 1: Murderous Home." For our entertainment. See https://www.amazon.com/Prison-Historical-Recordings-Parchman-1947-48/dp/B0000002UV.

26. Aucoin, Review of *Down on Parchman Farm*, 1.

A Theology of Justice

depicted in videos and lyrically; Murder Inc. Records and Death Row Records were two examples.

Art imitating life, or life imitating art, is an ongoing discussion. There is no question, however, of rap music's role in chronicling the relationship between the two. In an article for the American Bar Association titled "The Music of Mass Incarceration," the relationship is illuminated:

> And its importance is not limited to entertainment, capitalism, and economics. Indeed, rap has played a vital role in the documentation of mass incarceration. From its beginnings 50 years ago, hip hop has explored a range of themes that address the root causes and detrimental effects of mass incarceration, including urban decay, poverty, community violence, hyper-policing, police misconduct and brutality, government surveillance, tough-on-crime policies, and prosecutorial zeal.[27]

Ethic Thirteen—An effective corrections ethic must take seriously the assertion by Jean-Jacques Rousseau that "slaves lose everything in their chains, even the desire of escaping from them." Therefore an effective corrections ethic must devise through curricula, or other pedagogical instruments, and through therapeutic modalities, effective strategies for elucidating the phenomenon known as *internalized racist oppression*.

This can be implemented through inmate treatment plans, and required courses prescribed during the inmate intake assessment process. Donna Bivens, writing in *Flipping the Script: White Privilege and Community Building*, provides a definition of internalized racism.

> As people of color are victimized by racism, we internalize it. That is, we develop ideas, beliefs, actions and behaviors that support or collude with racism. This internalized racism has its own systemic reality and its own negative consequences in the lives and communities of people of color. More than just a consequence of racism, then, internalized racism is a systemic oppression

---

27. Dennis, "Music of Mass Incarceration," para. 5.

in reaction to racism that has a life of its own. In other words, just as there is a system in place that reinforces the power and expands the privilege of white people, there is a system in place that actively discourages and undermines the power of people and communities of color and mires us in our own oppression.[28]

W. E. B. Du Bois alluded to this phenomenon as *double consciousness*, to capture the distortion of Black life in America as a result of oppression and racism. Du Bois, writing in *The Souls of Black Folk*, explained this phenomenon further: "Du Bois used 'double consciousness' to refer to at least three different issues-including first the real power of white stereotypes in black life and thought and second the double consciousness created by the practical racism that excluded every black American from the mainstream of society."[29]

Today, the prison industrial complex, as it is referred to, has its conceptual roots as a business model in the convict lease system, and enterprises such as the Parchman Farm at the Mississippi State Prison. Like most exploitive systems of oppression stemming from earlier decades and centuries, the convict lease system and Parchman Farm have undergone a metamorphosis to a more sophisticated method of labor exploitation. The contemporary model of prison labor presents itself in the context of the innocuous sounding for-profit, prison privatization business model. Included also in this model is what Maryland and New Jersey once referred to as State Use Industries—now Maryland Correctional Enterprises.

While somewhat different from the jail and prison models to be examined under the for-profit, prison privatization, prison industrial complex models, it nonetheless is a means of revenue for the state by use of inmate labor. A 2005 Maryland News Release boasted its $39.86 million in revenue profits from the inmate workforce.

The basic premise of the success of the for-profit, prison privatization, prison industrial complex business model,

28. Bivens et al., "Flipping the Script," 44–45.
29. Du Bois, *Souls of Black Folk*, 238.

nonetheless, is as insidious as its predecessors. Unlike its predecessors, however, the for-profit, prison privatization, prison industrial complex is less repulsive to the casual uninformed observer. There are no overseers with shotguns on horses in the sweltering heat. Instead, the overseers of the for-profit, prison privatization, prison industrial complex are savvy corporate investors immersed in the culture of Wall Street and investing.

The significance of these correctional corporations are such that their identities bear restating here. The major corporations making up the for-profit, prison privatized, prison industrial complex are CoreCivic (formerly Corporation of America), and Geo Group (formerly Wackenhut Corrections) which is a multinational correctional corporation. Hence, the tentacles of the convict lease system are reprised well into the twentieth and twenty-first centuries.

As early as the nineties, the for-profit prison industry was having an impact on the financial markets. Jeff Sinden, writing in *Capitalist Punishment: Prison Privatization & Human Rights*, by Andrew Coyle, Allison Campbell, and Rodney Neufeld, documents the economic rise of the prison industrial complex:

> The private corrections industry quickly became a favorite on Wall Street. From an initial public offering price of $8 per share in 1995, the price of CCA stocks quadrupled in less than a year and hit highs of more than $100 in 1998 as investors were treated to skyrocketing share prices in the mid 1990's. While both have come down from their dizzying heights . . . they are still seen by experts as secure investments with excellent fundamentals: a recent report by the US Department of Justice estimates that annual total revenues for the industry are approximately $1 billion.[30]

From this, one need not be either an economist or a criminologist to comprehend that it is more profitable to maintain a prison population for economic gain, than to reintegrate inmates—ex-offenders—into society. No industry outside of corrections would

---

30. Sinden, "Problem of Prison Privatization," 44.

A History of Corrections in the United States

allow for such an obvious conflict in ethics. Due to the population of the for-profit, prison privatization, prison industrial complex services, there is a general tolerance by the public and the government to allow this glaring conflict of interest and violation of ethics.

The American Bar Association, of which I am a member, has moved this discussion from an ethical question to one of legality; questioning even the legality of for-profit, prison privatization, and the prison industrial complex outright. Sinden, writing again in *Capitalist Punishment: Prison Privatization & Human Rights*, says:

> One of the major features of the modern nation state is its monopoly on the legitimate use of violence and coercion in society. Only the state can detain, arrest and punish criminals.... The American Bar Association has pointed out that incarceration is an inherent function of the government and that the government should not abdicate this responsibility.[31]

Ethic Fourteen—An effective corrections ethic must affirm that the for-profit, prison privatization, prison industrial complex views human beings as commodities, or in social contract parlance *as means* to financial profitability, and not *as ends* toward personhood and dignity.

John Rawls suggests that human beings are to be treated in a manner reflective of justice, as if the rules were chosen by individuals themselves behind a *veil of ignorance*, in what is described as existing in an *original position*. In the original position, men and women would obviously agree to an arrangement in society, that would provide all interested persons with an equal starting point. The for-profit, prison privatization, prison industrial complex is an exploitation of entire communities, generations, and ethnic groups. These groups are viewed as expendable commodities, and serve as a means for increasing the value of Corrections Corporation of America (CoreCivic), Wackenhut Corrections (Geo

---

31. Sinden, "Problem of Prison Privatization," 44.

Group), further destabilizing a black and brown ecology, negating an equal starting point in society.

John Rawls writes in *A Theory of Justice*,

> Another way of putting this is to say that the principles of justice manifest in the basic structure of society men's desire to treat one another not as means only but as ends in themselves. . . . On the contract interpretation treating men as ends in themselves implies at the very least treating them in accordance with the principles to which they would consent in an original position of equality. For in this situation men have equal representation as moral persons who regard themselves as ends and the principles they accept will be rationally defined to protect the claims of their person. The contract view as such defines a sense in which men are to be treated as ends and not as means only. . . . To regard persons as ends in themselves in the basic design of society is to agree to forgo those gains which do not contribute to everyone's expectations.[32]

---

32. Rawls, *Theory of Justice*, 155–57.

Chapter 4

SOCIAL CONTRACT THEORY AS A BASIS FOR A CORRECTIONS ETHIC

ETHIC FIFTEEN—AN EFFECTIVE CORRECTIONS ethic must begin with an articulation of its rudimentary conception, of the essential character of persons relative to their potential for possessing the capacity for moral personality. This conception of the essential character of persons then should inform the policies and procedures, standard operating procedures, treatment and rehabilitative modalities for jails and prisons.

Corrections ethics should comprehend the essential character of inmates, then, in the tradition of John Locke which assumes the uniqueness of all human beings in their existence, which thereby inherently merits humane and dignified consideration, possessing *inalienable natural rights*.

Ethic Sixteen—An effective corrections ethic does not define the essential character of the inmate predicated upon the crime committed—no matter how heinous. An effective corrections ethic distinguishes between the essential character of the inmate, and the act or crime committed by the inmate.

A Theology of Justice

Therefore, the essential character of persons is understood as being in a *state of nature*, which possesses the potential for restoration to the state of being, prior to the development of criminogenic pathologies, and reflective of their potential in the original position.

Karl Barth, the preeminent Reformed theologian, reaffirms this *move* (in theology a move denotes a paradigm shift) in his *Church Dogmatics*,

> DeCou notes that for Barth . . . even if the prisoners had violated human law, the Church must be conscious of itself as a community entirely made up of convicted sinners who were only saved by the grace of God. Thus, the Church must be able to extend solidarity to all, not seeing a person as a good citizen or a convict . . . as a Christian or a non-Christian.[1]

Philosophers in the tradition of social contract theory help to establish the parameters defining the essential character of persons, or their original state of nature, prior to the establishing of the state or government. These philosophers most notably are John Locke, Thomas Hobbes, Jean-Jacques Rousseau, Immanuel Kant, and more recently John Rawls. In the most general context these philosophers are considered in the paradigm of contractarianism. *The Stanford Encyclopedia of Philosophy* defines contractarianism.

> The moral theory of contractarianism claims that moral norms derive their normative force from the idea of contract or mutual agreement. . . . Social contract theorists from the history of political thought include Hobbes, Locke, Kant, and Rousseau, [and] John Rawls, who effectively resurrected social contract theory in the second half of the 20th century.[2]

The value of John Locke to the conceptualization of men possessing value beyond their assigned status, and possessing an inherent self-worth, or natural rights, is immeasurable in the

---

1. Dhingra, "Karl Barth Visits Three Prisons," para. 16.
2. Cudd and Eftekhari, "Contractarianism," para. 1.

Social Contract Theory

history of thought relative to how we think of individual freedoms and rights. John Locke's thought on human rights is a cornerstone upon which civilized states have been shaped, or either despot states have rejected individual human rights; most notably influencing the Declaration of Independence.

The inspiration for the idea of *life, liberty and the pursuit of happiness* is undeniable in the writing of Thomas Jefferson, and attributed to the influence of John Locke. As one of the social contract theorists, John Locke's conceptualization of the social contract is not a theory of what an ideal relationship between man and authority would be like in an ideal world; however, it is a pragmatic scheme relative to that relationship in community. John Locke, writing in *Second Treatise of Government*, states the following:

> To understand political power right, and derive it from its original, we must consider, what state all men are naturally in, and that is, a state of perfect freedom to order their actions.... A state also of equality, wherein all the power and jurisdiction is reciprocal, no one having more than another ... no one ought to harm another in his life, health, liberty, or possessions.[3]

When the jail and prison industry as a whole is considered and understood as an ecosystem which influences the culture and society of which it is the environment, Locke's statements on the state of human liberties can thus be interpreted as a repudiation of the systemic and insidious process of incarceration in the United States—a process that marginalizes and restricts the liberties, freedoms, and development of individuals and whole communities through wholesale incarceration of the poor, the undereducated, persons of color, the seriously mentally ill, and those addicted to drugs and or alcohol.

Interpreting the essential character of persons is fundamental in determining the goal of corrections as a discipline. Previously, this corrections ethic has authenticated an ethic predicated upon

---

3. Locke, *Second Treatise of Government*, 2.4, 6.

A Theology of Justice

the premise of the essential character of persons possessing intrinsic self-worth. This ethic is juxtaposed with theoretical interpretations of the essential character of persons as lacking civility and potential for advanced development. This interpretation serves as the underpinning for a corrections discipline that focuses on a punitive conceptualization of jails and prisons. This conceptualization has its roots based in a Hobbesian interpretation of social contract theory. In Thomas Hobbes's model of social contract theory, the state of nature is understood far more pessimistically than for John Locke.

Hobbes understands man without the benefit of the state or government to be savage and lacking in civility. In Hobbes's interpretation of the social contract, he advocates that man be absolutely submissive to a sovereign power or authority. Thomas Hobbes articulates his view of the state of nature of man in his major publication titled *The Leviathan*:

> No Arts; no Letters; no Society; and which is worst of all, continual fear, and danger of violent death; And life of man, solitary, poor, nasty, brutish, and short. It may seem strange to some man, that has not well weighed these things; that Nature should thus dissociate, and render men apt to invade, and destroy one another.[4]

The punitive model of corrections intends to inflict a level of deficit upon the criminal offender for a variety of reasons. One reason is to exact a level of inconvenience upon the offender in a manner equivalent to the inconvenience experienced by the victim or the community of a particular crime. *Lex Talionis,* or the Law of Retaliation, shows up in early Mesopotamian laws and codes. It literally implies that an offender should receive the exact punishment which is reflective of the harm perpetrated upon the victim. It is an *eye for an eye* type of justice. It is the same conceptualization of punishment inherent in the Code of Hammurabi, which again justifies punishment in proportion to the crime committed.

---

4. Hobbes, *Leviathan*, 62.

Social Contract Theory

Punishment is also understood by some as a catharsis for society. By exacting punishment, somehow society is made whole. The punitive model of corrections fails in one significant goal, however. It fails to address the underlying cause(s) of the crime committed, or the maladaptive behavior underlying the offender's actions, nor does it cultivate techniques or skills for the offender to avoid future infractions. Obviously, this is not the intended goal(s) of adherents of the punitive model of corrections.

A Hobbesian approach to corrections contains or restricts the immediate danger posed by the offender, but arguably offers nothing beyond the remedy of the present crisis. It is shortsighted and offers little beyond a visceral sense of well-being. In a chapter titled "Persons and Punishment," by Herbert Morris, in the book *Punishment and Rehabilitation*, edited by Jeffries G. Murphy, the following observation is made:

> A person who violates the rules has something others have-the benefits of the system—but by renouncing what others have assumed, the burdens of self-restraint, he has acquired an unfair advantage. Matters are not even until this advantage is in some way erased.... Justice—that is, punishing such individuals—restores the equilibrium of benefits and burdens by ... exacting the debt.[5]

What is yet undetermined is what constitutes punishment? Arguably, punishment is removing an individual from society and isolating that individual in a correctional facility. Is this sufficient punishment? Does the punishment need to be more severe, such as placing offenders in restraint chairs, or placing offenders in solitary confinement for twenty-three hours per day? Is this sufficient punishment? Does punishment require the ending of the offender's life? More urgent, is punishment, the law, applied uniformly without regard to *social location* and without bias?

Ethic Seventeen—An effective corrections ethic does not imply that treatment or rehabilitation is the absence of punishment. Treatment and punishment are coterminous, as long as the

---

5. Murphy, *Punishment and Rehabilitation*, 76.

object of punishment serves to facilitate corrective behaviors, and not as a means to exact revenge upon the offender. The motivation behind the punishment is just as important as the imposing of punitive measures in an effective corrections ethic.

Punishment should never be the arbitrary use of intimidation by correctional personnel, indiscriminately employing its use to dehumanize inmates within jails and prisons. Punishment must have a methodology. Punitive measures must be well prepared, and conceived in a therapeutic and controlled setting, thereby eliminating or minimizing its use or conception during the *fog of war*, when abuses of punishment are almost certain.

Ethic Eighteen—An effective corrections ethic affirms the essential belief that individuals are capable of reform or rehabilitation, from criminogenic tendencies inculcated through their environment. Offenders are able to develop behaviors and skills through comprehensive education curricula, and therapeutic modalities in order to be successfully reintegrated into the community, or able to achieve the least restrictive security classification, ranging from maximum security classification, to a medium security classification, to a minimum security classification, to finally reintegration into the community in an *aftercare* model.

Social contract theorist Jean-Jacques Rousseau affirmed through his work *The Social Contract* the prominence of freedom and liberty as a central motif. Rousseau believed that individuals possess agency or autonomy relative to their destiny and can make choices that reflect this freedom. Unlike animals that are destined to be controlled through nature or instincts, human beings can engineer their own journey. This is particularly important in the formation of corrections ethics, and its emphasis upon rehabilitation.

Writing in the *Stanford Encyclopedia of Philosophy* in an article titled "Jean-Jacques Rousseau," Chris Bertram, a professor of social and political philosophy at the University of Bristol, highlights Rousseau's emphasis upon freedom:

> Rousseau regards the capacity for choice, and therefore the ability to act against instinct and inclination, as one

Social Contract Theory

of the features that distinguishes the human race from animal species and makes truly moral action possible. In the *Discourse on the Origins of Inequality* . . . he characterizes animal species . . . as mechanisms programmed to a fixed behavior.[6]

Further complicating life for humanity is the reality according to Rousseau, that society is contrived in such a way as to compound the debilitating conditions that tend to marginalize individuals, and favor conditions that preserve the status of those in control. Rousseau argued that these conditions were established early in the formation of society, as individuals made untenable claims to property and possessions. In a translation by G. D. H. Cole titled, *A Discourse for the Academy of Dijon*, Cole highlights Rousseau's indignation concerning civil society. Rousseau famously wrote in *Discourse on the Origins of Inequality*:

> The first man who, having fenced in a piece of land, said, "This is mine," and found people naïve enough to believe him, that man was the true founder of civil society. From how many crimes, wars, and murders, from how many horrors and misfortunes might not any one have saved mankind, by pulling up the stakes, or filling up the ditch, and crying to his fellows: Beware of listening to this impostor; you are undone if you once forget that the fruits of the earth belong to us all, and the earth itself to nobody.[7]

The demography of jails and prisons at the state and county level in the United States are disproportionately made up of individuals lacking property, position, and power. There is a correlative relationship between poverty and incarceration. It is obvious that the poor do not commit more crimes than do the wealthy; however, they are more likely to encounter discriminatory practices throughout the adjudication process from beginning to end. Writing in *Inequality: Social Class and Its Consequences*, edited by D. Stanley Eitzen and Janis E. Johnston, Jeffrey Riemann observes the

---

6. Bertram, "Jean-Jacques Rousseau," para. 26.
7. Rousseau, *Discourse for the Academy of Dijon*, Part II.

following. "Between crimes that are characteristically committed by poor people (street crimes) and those characteristically committed by the well-off (white collar and corporate crimes), the system treats the former much more harshly than the latter, even when the crimes of the well-off take more money from the public or cause more death and injury than the crimes of the poor."[8]

Ethic Nineteen—An effective corrections ethic interprets the correlation between disparities in wealth, or what Rawls refers to as primary goods, and the dissolution of order or civility within society, to the extent that individuals are excluded from participating in upward mobility, and the quality of life certain others are readily afforded due to the advantage of social location. The resulting effect of this debilitating correlation is the criminalization of entire communities and the branding of its citizens, African American youth in particular, as outlaws.

One of the most deleterious practices or strategies to continue the hegemonic marginalization of Black and Brown communities—communities comprised often of ex-offenders—is the practice of making the ex-offender unemployable. Unemployment is de facto standard practice in civil society, the public sector, and private sector, affecting ex-offenders and their ability to enjoy the dignity of rearing a family, of decent housing, and what Rawls refers to as the primary goods in society. The right to work has such urgent implications that the Universal Declaration of Human Rights has identified it in Article 23(3): "Everyone . . . is entitled to realization . . . of the economic, social and cultural rights indispensable for his dignity." Finally, in connection with the right to work in Article 23(3), the Declaration claims that "Everyone who works has the right to just and favorable enumeration ensuring for himself and his family an existence worthy of human dignity."[9]

Ex-offenders must have the right to stable and long-term employment. Legislation to incentivize hiring practices is a mechanism to disrupt ex-offender employment apartheid and to decouple the ex-offender from excessive fees paid for probation

---

8. Eitzen and Johnson, *Inequality*, 145.
9. Shelton, *Oxford Handbook*, 347.

and parole supervision. It is a never ending cycle of poverty and debt.

In a book review for the School of Theology Center for Practical Theology at Boston University, the significance of work as a theology is highlighted. In *Theology of Work* by Darrell Cosden, it is noted that some of the most influential figures have expounded upon a theology of work. "Miroslav Volf's Work in the Spirit, Karl Marx's views on work and ontology, the Papal encyclical 'Laborem Exercens' by Pope John Paul II. There are also various small treatments on work by Martin Luther, John Calvin, Karl Barth, and Dietrich Bonhoeffer that Cosden draws from."[10]

If work is a theological construct as well as an economic construct, it must follow that work is a *moral imperative*—and therefore considered a human right. The right of ex-offenders to work is a moral imperative. Impediments to work must be seen as a violation of *human* rights—a violation of *natural* rights.

Social contract theorist John Rawls articulates three concepts imperative to an effective corrections ethic, relative to the aforementioned disparity in wealth and the dissolution of civility within society: *two principles of justice, primary goods,* and *conception of reciprocity*.

The two principles of justice Rawls envisions in *A Theory of Justice* do not extract wealth or property from the wealthy and redistribute them to the indigent; however, they create an environment of opportunity and access by all to the most comprehensive range of prospects. "First: each person is to have an equal right to the most extensive scheme of equal basic liberties compatible with a similar scheme of liberties for others. Second: social and economic inequalities are to be arranged so that they are both (a) reasonably expected to be to everyone's advantage, and (b) attached to positions and offices open to all."[11]

The two principles of justice would effectively create a more equitable society, thereby affording alternatives to criminogenic life choices and allowing marginalized individuals and dislocated

---

10. Sweden, Review of *Theology of Work*, para. 3.
11. Rawls, *Theory of Justice*, 53.

communities to participate in quality-of-life opportunities heretofore made inaccessible to them. This structural change, accompanied with the dismantling of the systemic strategy to incarcerate certain segments of society, would dramatically reduce the rate of incarceration and the jail and prison population.

Rawls contends that there are basic possessions each person in society can reasonably expect to desire. These he references as *primary goods*.

> Suppose that the basic structure of society distributes certain primary goods, that is, things that every rational man is presumed to want. These goods normally have a use whatever a person's rational plan of life. For simplicity, assume that the chief primary goods at the disposition of society are rights, liberties, and opportunities, and income and wealth. These are the social primary goods.[12]

Rawls argues that a just society comprehends the *mutual benefit* of all parties in a given society having parity and material goods. This need not be predicated upon the altruism of those in society who possess power, wealth, and property; however, it can be understood as a means for achieving and maintaining stability within a given society. It is most often a lesson lost on those who wield power, not only in despot countries but those in power within the United States. The egregious uneven distribution of wealth and power, within institutions of law and financial markets, as well as higher education access, destabilizes the country as a whole, as evidenced by the financial crisis and the housing market crash of the last two decades. This is indicative of a minority of interested parties accumulating and hoarding wealth at the expense of the larger society.

Rawls contends,

> The difference principle expresses a conception of reciprocity. It is a principle of mutual benefit. . . . Thus the more advantaged, when they view the matter from a general perspective, recognize that the well-being of each depends on a scheme of social cooperation without

---

12. Rawls, *Theory of Justice*, 54.

which no one could have a satisfactory life; they recognize also that they can expect the willing cooperation of all only if the terms of the scheme are reasonable.[13]

Ethic Twenty—An effective corrections ethic corroborates the theories posited by both Rousseau and Rawls, and the implications that social stratification portends, creates and maintains a permanent underclass and jail and prison population, through the systematic implementation of policies, rules and regulations, which serve as hegemonic strategies that erode the quality of life, dignity, and ethical judgment of *racialized communities.*

Corrections ethics has a fundamental goal, the deciphering of such strategies to communities most adversely impacted, and to develop practices and strategies to circumvent unfair rules, laws, and cultural biasness. This can be accomplished via the academy, community organizing, and the Black Church, as well as all concerned with social justice and understanding the role of theology and law.

---

13. Rawls, *Theory of Justice*, 88.

Chapter 5

ENVIRONMENTAL FACTORS LEADING TO JAIL AND PRISON

ETHIC TWENTY-ONE—AN EFFECTIVE CORRECTIONS ethic must analyze and incorporate into programs, curricula, policies and procedures, and standard operating procedures a methodology that interprets the context-ethos of environmental factors that lead to jail and prison.

To say that poverty, jail and prison are coterminous is not hyperbole. Poverty is one of the most determinative variables pertinent to choices, and the lack thereof in the lives of people ensnared in the cycle of poverty. As well, poverty is often misunderstood by those who have had the good fortune of resources, access, and entry into a reality of opportunities. This misconception of poverty weighed heavily upon the social consciousness of the social activist and cofounder of the *Catholic Worker* (an influential publication focused on social justice), Dorothy Day. Day, writing in *On Poverty*, illuminates this misconception.

> We must talk about poverty because people lose sight of it, can scarcely believe that it exists. So many decent people come in to visit us and tell us how their families were brought up in poverty and how, through hard work and decent habits and cooperation, they managed to

Environmental Factors Leading to Jail and Prison

educate all the children and raise up priests and nuns to the Church. They concede that health and good habits, a good family, take them out of the poverty class, no matter how mean the slum they may have been forced to inhabit. No, they don't know about the poor. Their conception of poverty is something neat and well ordered as a nun's cell.[1]

The social contract theory as espoused by John Rawls introduces two concepts that take environmental variables into consideration. The first Rawls refers to as the *morality of authority* and it is a concept that suggests that children develop a sense of morality first in the family. While the presumption is that the morality inculcated within the child through the family will make for a well-adjusted individual, the same holds true for values which represent countercultural mores. In either instance, these values are learned and developed by children through the institution of the family.

Rawls outlines the morality of authority in a *Theory of Justice*:

> The first stage in the sequence of moral development I shall refer to as the morality of authority. . . . We can regard the morality of authority in its primitive form as that of the child. I assume that the sense of justice is acquired gradually by the younger members of society as they grow up. . . . The necessity to teach moral attitudes (however simple) to children is one of the conditions of human life.[2]

Ethic Twenty-Two—An effective corrections ethic deconstructs the pathologies associated with the fracture of the family unit, and the criminogenic lifestyle internalized through the *succession of generations*, and the resultant contributing factors leading to the criminalization of individuals and whole communities.

The second concept introduced by Rawls and imperative for an effective corrections ethic is the *morality of association*. *Ethic Twenty-Three*— The morality of association refers to the

1. Day, *On Poverty*, 2.
2. Rawls, *Theory of Justice*, 405.

71

community of which an individual is most influenced subsequent to the family. Because individuals do not exist in a vacuum, the influence of the environment upon the behavior of the individual cannot be overstated. The case can be made arguably that the societal norms and mores of a given community can supersede even the influence of familial structures. Therefore, corrections ethics must advocate for intervention in the communities most severely affected by criminogenic patterns prior to, throughout, and post incarceration.

Rawls defines the morality of association in *A Theory of Justice*:

> The second stage of moral development is that of the morality of association. This stage covers a wide range of cases depending on the association in question and it may even include the national community as a whole. . . . The content of the morality of association is given by the moral standards appropriate to the individual's role in the various associations to which he belongs. These standards include the common sense rules of morality along with the adjustment required to fit them to a person's particular position; and they are impressed upon him by the approval and disapproval of those in authority, or by the other members of the group. . . . Similarly there is the association of the school and the neighborhood, and also such short-term forms of cooperation, though not less important for this, as games and play with peers.[3]

An effective corrections ethic understands the *morality of association* as influential and formative, relative to the community and its impression upon the *tabula rasa* of individuals. This holds true then not only in a healthy, constructive well-adjusted context, but also in a debilitating construct as well. Therefore, corrections ethics must interpret the morality of association and its impact, upon communities and individuals in the context of jail and prison incarceration trends.

---

3. Rawls, *Theory of Justice*, 409.

Environmental Factors Leading to Jail and Prison

Too often the discussion centered on incarceration, jails, and prisons in the United States is misconstrued to convey that the majority of African Americans are representative of the population within penal institutions. To be more exact, African Americans representative of the lower socioeconomic strata within the United States disproportionately are incarcerated at a higher rate than other groups. Arguably, poorer African Americans relative to incarceration serve as a bellwether for the state of race relations, the state of the economy, and the fate of poorer uneducated whites, and other minority groups in the United States.

However, this dangerous misnomer within the American consciousness is that African Americans are monolithic, and that jails and prisons are overpopulated with African Americans representative of every social location. This consciousness is void of any interpretation, reflective of the social location of African American upwardly mobile communities, the Black intelligentsia or successful Black entrepreneurs. This is evidenced by the heightened awareness of many African Americans who have had the occasion of an encounter with law enforcement in the context of ordinary traffic law enforcement, who are well aware of white America's suspicion and fear of radicalized constructs of the lawless Black, and fear this perception invites escalation. This was the case with Harvard University Professor Dr. Louis Gates, who was arrested at his home near the Harvard Campus in 2009 for being *suspicious.*

Seared in the consciousness of many Americans is the evening news depicting African Americans being arrested by the police for drug activity, or for some heinous street level hooliganism. Many Americans are not discerning enough to discriminate between well-educated and poorer educated African Americans. In a utopian society this distinction would not necessitate identification. It is important, however, to make this distinction when writing a corrections ethic, which by necessity will explore many topics heretofore exploited and misrepresented in the public square. As the author of a corrections ethic which extrapolates from social contract theory as espoused by John Rawls, I am careful not to perpetuate derogatory images and stereotypes, readily available for the affirmation of xenophobic assumptions.

Lawrence Otis Graham chronicled the stealth world of the African American elite in his book titled *Our Kind of People: Inside America's Black Upper Class*. In a book review by Harper Perennial Graham describes life in this community.

> Debutante cotillions. Million-dollar homes. Summers in Martha's Vineyard. Membership in the Links, Jack and Jill, Deltas, Boule, and AKAs. An obsession with the right schools, families, social clubs, and skin complexion. This is the world of the black upper class and the focus of the first book written about the black elite by a member of this hard-to-penetrate group.[4]

Having delineated the parameters of black life in the United States, a conscientious corrections ethic investigates the experiences which are juxtaposed with the African American elite and upper middle class; primarily, those representing the socioeconomically marginalized group of African Americans of which this corrections ethic is particularly engaged.

As a director for the Maryland Division of Pretrial Detention and Services from 1992 through 2007, I began to observe a disturbing trend within the correctional facility. During this time, the correctional facility began housing inmates that were often related to each other, and at times from the same immediate family. It was not uncommon to have a mother housed in the WDC building or Women's Detention Center, a son in the Juvenile section of the facility, and a father in the MDC building or Men's Detention Center. Over a period of years, correctional personnel would begin to recognize younger offenders, as a result of knowing the father or an uncle who had passed through the system years before. The cycle of incarceration was being perpetuated from one generation to yet another generation. The criminogenic psychosis of the family was being internalized and retaught either subconsciously or intentionally. I refer to this phenomenon as *legacy correctional*

---

4. See the synopsis for Graham, *Our Kind of People*.

Environmental Factors Leading to Jail and Prison

institutionalization to describe the transmission of criminogenic values within families or whole communities.

In many communities, the morality of authority is a familial system which passes down values, and reflects an ethos in conflict with or antithetical to mainstream American values. This same ethos parallels the pervasive culture of jails and prisons in the United States. In certain communities children learn that the jail and prison is a place to be visited on a weekly basis, much in the same manner some children grow up with the synagogue, mosque, or parish being a part of their orientation.

As a director, I often recalled visiting lines that stretched extensively down the sidewalk at the detention center, filled with mothers and babies waiting to enter the correctional facility. Even at the earliest stages of my career, I was astute enough to query concerning the danger of familiarizing young children, with the day-to-day routine of incorporating the jail into their familial paradigm. In the case of the Maryland Division of Pretrial Detention and Services, it was an institution which was a part of a larger complex or consortium of jails and prisons. This complex of penal institutions was within the community of East Baltimore, and was situated between the communities of East Baltimore and the downtown business district of Baltimore City.

The deleterious impact of the physical location of the facility, is that its presence is inescapable if you live in East Baltimore. The complex consisted of the Maryland Division of Pretrial Detention and Services; the former Maryland State Penitentiary where the death penalty is carried out; the Maryland Super Maximum Prison for the most notorious criminals, housing such infamous individuals as Lee Boyd Malvo, half of the DC sniper pair, who carried out random killings in the Maryland and District of Columbia area between October 2, 2002, and October 24, 2002; and the Central Booking facility which was technically a part of the Maryland Division of Pretrial Detention and Services.

This consortium of jails and prisons must be negotiated by children going to and from school, or downtown Baltimore City, and is a blight on both the physical and mental landscape of the children and adults of the East Baltimore community. This correctional complex would never exist in communities possessing political clout or the luxury of choices. One would never choose to live in a community that served as a daily reminder, of the lack of opportunities and the drudgery of life one can look forward to.

In 2003, during my tenure, *The New York Times* chronicled the life of a young girl growing up in the shadow of the jail and prison maze. In an article titled "Prison Is a Member of Their Family," Adrian Nicole LeBlanc captured the experience.

> Since Nina was born, Lolli has been dressing her for prison. Nina wore new baby clothes for visits to her 16-year old father, Toney, in a juvenile detention facility not too far from their Bronx neighborhood. As Nina grew, Lolli dressed her daughter for the rarer afternoons in faraway New York State maximum-security visiting rooms. . . .
>
> On a cold morning early last month, Nina, who is now 12, stood on her stoop, dressed, waiting to visit her father. . . . She has been an upstate girl for more than seven years. . . .
>
> As long as Nina could remember, the prison system held uncles and cousins and grandfathers and always her father. Nina, like Toney and Lolli, was raised in the inner city; for all three, prison further demarcated the already insular social geography. Along with the baby shower of teenagers, they attended prisoners' going-away and coming-home parties. . . . Corrections officers escorted one handcuffed cousin to Nina's great-grandmother's funeral; her favorite uncle had to be unshackled in order to approach his dying grandmother's hospital bedside. The prison system was part of the texture of family life.[5]

Ethic Twenty-Four—An effective corrections ethic must devise methodologies, mechanisms centered not on helping individuals to escape the so-called ghettos, or communities mired in despair for the suburbs, as this is not pragmatic; rather, the goal must be to inundate these communities with evidence-based collaborations.

---

5. LeBlanc, "Prison Is a Member of Their Family," paras. 1–2.

Environmental Factors Leading to Jail and Prison

Perhaps it is possible to realize a pedagogy of theology reflective of transvaluation, in the context of transforming urban blight. As I wrote in *Thirteen Turns: A Theology Resurrected from the Gallows of Jim Crow Christianity* concerning transvaluation:

> The dialectic of the cross is the transvaluation of defeat, and the whole of the Beatitudes of Jesus rendered in the Sermon on the Mount. Each tenet of the Beatitudes is a transvaluation of human understanding, and everything counterintuitive to what society deems as strong. Reinhold Niebuhr characterized the whole of Christianity in the context of transvaluation. "Or as Niebuhr put it, The Christian Faith is centered in one who was born in a manger and who dies upon the cross. This is really the source of the Christian transvaluation of all values."[6]

A pedagogy of theology, reflective of transvaluation for decimated urban blighted communities can be grounded in the Hebrew Biblical text in Jeremiah.

> This is what the Lord Almighty, the God of Israel, says to all those I carried into exile from Jerusalem to Babylon: 'Build houses and settle down; plant gardens and eat what they produce. Marry and have sons and daughters; find wives for your sons and give your daughters in marriage, so that they too may have sons and daughters. Increase in number there; do not decrease. Also, seek the peace and prosperity of the city to which I have carried you into exile, Pray to the Lord for it, because if it prospers, you too will prosper.[7]

Life in the shadows of the East Baltimore communities surrounded by the consortium of jails and prisons is an exile. Not an exile informed by divine manipulation, but an exile informed by egregious urban planning, failing schools, politics of fear, and racism fueled by political demagoguery. Transform these communities into inclusive centers of life. Not gentrification, not removal of the poor farther into despair, but a transformation with its goal

---

6. Covin, *Thirteen Turns*, 53.
7. Jer 29: 4–7 (NIV).

of restructuring the hope, imagination, and conceptualization of people indigenous to urban communities.

Partnerships between businesses and schools represent possible collaborations. Other potential alliances between local colleges and universities with at-risk communities are necessary to negate communities being drawn into the criminogenic vortex. Paradoxically, the jail and prison can act as a de facto university, where offenders learn the most basic educational and life skills missed in the formation of their morality of authority. Presently, most jails and prisons are universities for honing criminal activities.

Religious institutions must also be informed participants in the collaborative equation of community and institutions. This is particularly true within the context of the African American community, in which the church serves as a surrogate family for many single women, children, and young men who are often recruited for illicit entrepreneurial prospectives. In certain communities the institutional Black Church is one of the few, if not only, settings families can go to that have any semblance of structure, and is a locus of respect, power, and influence in the community.

Writing in "Faith among Black Americans" for the Pew Research Center the following observation is made. "Black pastors hold a storied place in American history. During the eras of slavery and racial segregation, they played pivotal roles in Black communal efforts to "uplift the race" (a phrase commonly used in the 19th and 20th centuries). This often included organizing job training, after-school mentoring, insurance collectives, athletic clubs and other community service programs through their churches[and] leading protests against racial discrimination."[8] Corrections ethics must engage every resource available, to disrupt the heritage of Legacy Correctional Institutionalization within marginalized communities.

Central to an effective corrections ethic is the initiation of advocacy throughout each phase of the adjudicatory process, by encouraging the stability of the familial structure. Consistent with high rates of incarceration is the erosion of a significant family

---

8. "Faith among Black Americans," para. 1.

Environmental Factors Leading to Jail and Prison

unit support system. The culture of jails and prisons as reflected in their policies and procedures, standard operating procedures, and inmate handbooks need to incorporate practices and mechanisms that support strong family involvement with offenders in order to reduce recidivism.

Programming that instructs offenders on building and maintaining healthy relationships is a viable approach to this end. Creating a morality of authority paradigm that inculcates family members, with values consistent with those of the larger society, corrections ethics must engage the challenges that exist which continually decimate the family unit and marginalize communities. This is of particular concern within the demographic of the African American community, of which this corrections ethic is particularly concerned.

There are competing and divergent theories related to the dissolution of the family within black culture, none of which, however, deny the catastrophic impact this has had on the overall wellness of black culture in America. As Rawls has postulated in his morality of authority, it is within the context of the family that children learn how to exist in the larger context of society. It is within this context that children learn what is normative and tend to replicate learned values in their lives.

The absence of the male figure in African American homes is detrimental in many instances. Identifying this phenomenon runs the risk of being accused of misogyny; as it has become a significant nexus of contention within certain circles of the Black community. Practically speaking, the economic impact of missing fathers is traumatic and creates a financial hardship upon families. The emotional strain of rearing children as a single parent is unhealthy for both the child as well as the adult in highly stressful communities. While this phenomenon may appear trendy, and even a sign of independence and liberation for women in higher socioeconomic communities, it has proven to undermine and threaten the stability of the African American community. This trend has persisted over the last several decades. Roberta L. Coles, associate professor of sociology at Marquette University, and

A THEOLOGY OF JUSTICE

Charles Green, professor of sociology at Hunter College (at the time of this writing) describe the magnitude of the problem in *The Myth of the Missing Black Father*.

The introduction of Coles and Green's *The Myth of the Black Father* highlights alarming statistics:

> Only 16 percent of African American households were married couples with children, the lowest of all racial groups in America. On the other hand, 19 percent of Black households were female-headed with children, the highest of all racial groups. From the perspective of children's living arrangements over 50 percent of African American children lived in mother-only households in 2004, again the highest of all racial groups. Although African American teens experienced the largest decline of births of all racial groups in the 1990s, still in 2000, 68 percent of all births to African American women were non-marital suggesting the pattern of single-mother parenting may be sustained for some time into the future.[9]

Although this statistical analysis does not give insight into the phenomenon of cohabitating relationships, in terms of boyfriends or live-in partners, this latter paradigm further reinforces what is normative for children growing up in these domiciles, and thus a predictor of future boyfriend or cohabitating relationships as the norm. Thus, a corrections ethic that advocates the stabilization of families through the traditional institution of marriage is concerned less with the question of morality in this instance, and is focused more upon the quantifiable benefits of married households.

Writing in an article titled "Studies Find Big Benefits in Marriage," Jennifer Steinhauer includes the findings of Dr. Linda Waite, the George Herbert Mead Distinguished Service Professor of Sociology at The University of Chicago as of this writing.

> A body of demographic research presented at the conference of the Population Association of America here today indicated that marriage offers dramatic emotional,

---

9. Coles and Green, *Myth of the Missing Black Father*, 1.

Environmental Factors Leading to Jail and Prison

> financial and even health benefits over the single life and cohabitation....
>
> An enhanced commitment that comes naturally with marriage, she said, increases all levels of support that individuals bring to their relationship and lives. Cohabitation does not generally imply a lifetime commitment to stay together, she said. Cohabitants are more likely to assume that each partner is responsible for supporting him or herself....
>
> Dr. Waite, a professor of sociology at the University of Chicago whose research focuses on family structure, drew from various resources in her work, including the National Survey of Families and Households, [and] a sampling of 13,000 adults.[10]

In corrections, I have witnessed trends introduced and abandoned over nearly twenty years within jails and prisons. Some projects have had great promise and were influenced by evidence based research. Others were ill-conceived and anecdotal. There is a balance to be achieved between programming which is bold and innovative, and that which is debilitating to the inmate population.

The Baltimore City Detention Center, in an effort to combat the epidemic of heroine use in Baltimore, instituted the Addicts Changing Together Substance Abuse Program at the jail, introducing the technique of acupuncture among the inmate population. Mary Stewart, the program director during the time of its employment, made the following observation.

> Stewart said anecdotal evidence suggests the acupuncture treatments have reduced stress levels among addicts and helped them regain control of their bodily functions. But Stewart admitted prison officials have no research-based evidence that acupuncture, taken alone and out of context from the program's other services, has any real effect in helping the addicts' recovery.[11]

---

10. Steinhauer, "Studies Find Big Benefits in Marriage," paras. 2, 4–5.
11. Hyland, "City Jail Acupuncture Program in Doubt," 1.

One such program which attempted to address the poverty-broken family nexus was the now-defunct Oklahoma Marriage Initiative, ended in 2016. In Oklahoma, the controversial program referred to as the Oklahoma Marriage Initiative collaborated with the Oklahoma Department of Corrections to create a prison based curriculum that sought to strengthen marriages and relationships of prisoners. The program workshops allowed for inmates to participate in individual sessions as well as couple's sessions when practical. Writing in an article for the US Department of Health and Human Services, titled "Marriage and Relationship Skills Education as a Way to Prepare Prisoners for Reintegration," researchers made the following justification:

> High rates of incarceration have fueled interest in services to reduce recidivism. . . . Oklahoma's Department of Corrections (DOC) began to focus on reentry programs to better prepare inmates for release and to reduce recidivism. To explore whether relationships and marriage education might improve inmates' ability to return to and maintain viable marriages upon release.[12]

Though controversial and now defunct, an effective corrections ethic incorporates within its programs the best practices related to strengthening of the family unit, less a moral imperative and more as a methodology and mechanism to reduce recidivism, such as the Oklahoma Marriage Initiative experiment with the Oklahoma Department of Corrections.

As the director of treatment at the Adams County Adult Correctional Complex in Gettysburg, Pennsylvania, I realized the enormity of the impact of environmental factors leading to incarceration, as the majority of offenders presented with drug and alcohol addiction, and lacked high school diplomas. The correlation between incarceration and education attainment is a historic trend, and is documented over decades. As I have written in *Thirteen Turns: A Theology Resurrected From the Gallows of Jim Crow Christianity*: "Caroline Wolf Harlow writing in an article titled

---

12. Dion et al., "Marriage and Relationship Skills Education," para. 5.

Environmental Factors Leading to Jail and Prison

"Education and Correctional Populations," makes the following observation. 'About 41% of inmates in the Nation's State and Federal prisons and local jails in 1997 and 31% of probationers had not completed high school or its equivalent. In comparison, 18% of the general population age 18 or older had not finished the 12th grade.'"[13]

Unlike the Division of Pretrial Detention and Services, located in East Baltimore whose inmates had a high rate of addiction to both heroin and crack cocaine, the inmates at the Adams County Adult Correctional Complex, presented with a high rate of addiction to alcohol and meth or methamphetamine. Different environments produced different addictions. Further, time has given us the lens to also understand, that often a certain demographic will identify with a particular drug of choice; frequently the corresponding drug with a particular community, will elicit a judicial and societal response commensurate with that community's social location.

This phenomenon is captured in an article titled "Comparing Black and White Drug Offenders: Implications for Racial Disparities in Criminal Justice and Reentry Policy and Programming," by Alana Rosenberg of the Yale School of Public Health, Allison Groves of the Dornsife School of Public Health at Drexel University, and Kim Blankenship of American University.

> The overwhelming increase in incarceration, attributed to the drug war, has disproportionately impacted Black communities. In 2011, Blacks were incarcerated at a dramatically higher rate than Whites (5–7 times) and accounted for almost half of all prisoners incarcerated with a sentence of more than one year for a drug-related offense.[14]

In short, often African American addiction is criminalized, while White American addiction is interpreted as a treatment necessity; hence the opioid crisis response juxtaposed with the crack crisis response. Dr. Jessica Isom of the Yale School of

13. Covin, *Thirteen Turns*, 77–78.
14. Rosenberg et al., "Comparing Black and White Drug Offenders," para. 2.

A Theology of Justice

Medicine, in an article titled "Race and the Criminalization of Drugs" by Chris Adams, identifies this response: "History itself demonstrates that there is a direct line between how we criminalize addiction and then how that loop results in a racialization of substance use."[15]

John Rawls articulates the impact of environmental influences external to the family unit, which have significant ramifications in the formation of community structures, vis-à-vis the morality of association. Individuals living in environments inundated with drug and alcohol abuse are more susceptible to addiction. The influence of peers, neighbors, and schools where drugs may be used recreationally, may act as predictors for future substance abuse.

Two environmental factors leading to incarceration are abuse of and addiction to drugs and or alcohol, and failure to receive a basic high school education. The correlation between addiction and crime is significant, and is often the catalyst for career criminals or those who have extensive criminal records, and recidivate at a high level. Crimes such as prostitution are often related to an offender engaging in their illegal activity in order to finance their drug habit. Property crimes such as shoplifting and burglary are often the result of addicts attempting to finance their habit.

When I served for a very brief period as executive director of Addiction Recovery Systems in Lancaster, Pennsylvania, a treatment facility for heroin-addicted patients, I witnessed the correlation between addiction and delinquent behaviors fueled by addiction to heroin. Patients seeking treatment at the clinic represented those who were in recovery, but also making progress toward living crime free as a consequence of *getting clean*. In many instances, once drugs and alcohol are removed from the equation, individuals discontinue in the criminal justice system. During my tenure in treatment and corrections, I have witnessed the havoc addiction has inflicted upon individuals and entire families, as well as their communities. Consequently, my approach to treatment is more pragmatic, aimed at addressing the various addictions.

15. Adams, "Race and the Criminalization of Drugs," para. 1.

Environmental Factors Leading to Jail and Prison

Ethic Twenty-Five—An effective corrections ethic should incorporate all, or any three, of the recommended treatment modalities to follow in order to disrupt the correlation between addiction and incarceration.

A best practice of some jails and prisons in the United States is the use of the therapeutic community or TC model. The TC model is an attempt to saturate the environment of the inmate during incarceration with strategies and tools for recovery. Writing in *Treating Addicted Offenders: A Continuum of Effective Practices*, Dr. Kevin Knight and Dr. David Farabee outline the premise of the therapeutic community model. "The TC philosophy regards substance abuse as a disorder of the whole person. Rather than being regarded as a disease, substance abuse and addiction are perceived as a symptom of a larger disorder that encompasses the users' values, cognitions, social skills, and general behavior."[16]

In a report titled "Multi-Site Evaluation of Prison-Based Drug Treatment: A Research Partnership Between the Pennsylvania Department of Corrections and Temple University," an excerpt of the Executive Summary by Dr. Wayne N. Welsh concluded the following.

> It is generally agreed that a multisite therapeutic community treatment continuum (TCTC) for drug offenders (e.g., TC treatment in prison, followed by transitional TC in a work-release setting, followed by supervision and aftercare treatment in the community) is associated with significant reductions in drug use and crime for up to 5 years after prison release. This evidence-based intervention has become the dominant paradigm for treating drug dependent inmates. Our results support evidence regarding the efficacy of this approach, but also highlight some pressing needs for further research.[17]

The second component of treatment advocated by this corrections ethic, albeit tepidly, is the use of methadone to treat heroin addiction. My initial resistance to methadone treatment was

---

16. Farabee and Knight, *Treating Addicted Offenders*, 30–32.
17. Welsh, "Multi-Site Evaluation of Prison-Based Drug Treatment," 6.

based largely in part upon individuals I experienced in Baltimore, who would exhibit what is referred to as *nodding* while in public spaces. At that time, my education in methadone was based upon anecdotal observation as opposed to methodological or systematic research. The Division of Pretrial Detention and Services was inundated with heroin abusers. This addicted population represents those individuals who had obviously failed in their struggle to free themselves of heroin addiction.

This population represents those inmates who continue to enter and exit the criminal justice system, due to their addiction or crimes committed directly related to their addiction. As the executive director of Addiction Recovery Systems, I encountered heroin addicts who were acting responsibly by treating their heroin addiction with either methadone or soboxone, both of which are treatments for opiate addiction. The difficult reality for many theorists or purists to accept is that some people will never be able to extricate themselves from the grasp of heroin addiction. Too often advocates, though well-intended, assert that because they were able to discontinue use of heroin, then others can do the same. Addiction is a different experience for each individual. While certainly not a panacea, treating heroin addiction with methadone significantly reduces the transmission of HIV/AIDS through needle sharing associated with heroin, dramatically reduces crime-related activities associated with heroin addiction, and removes the addicted individual from the criminal justice system because taking heroin is against the law, while taking methadone is not.

Therefore, a responsible and pragmatic corrections ethic advocates the use of methadone as a viable alternative to heroin addiction. "Methadone is one component of a comprehensive treatment plan, which includes counseling and other behavioral health therapies to provide patients with a whole-person approach."[18]

The third component of treatment advocated by this corrections ethic is that of spirituality. Like other forms of treatment, spirituality may be more helpful for some while not practical for others fighting addiction. Arguably, the role of either religion or

18. "Methadone," para. 3.

spirituality as a treatment modality, or as an aid in recovery, may be enhanced or negated by the conceptualization of the individual's metaphysics or ontological perspective. For offenders presenting with drug and or alcohol addiction, religion or spirituality serves as an additional resource from which to draw, if in fact their metaphysical or ontological perspective affirms a transcendent presence external to themselves. Writing an article titled "Religious Faith and Spirituality in Substance Abuse Recovery: Determining the Mental Health Benefits" in the *Journal of Substance Abuse Treatment*, the authors concluded the following:

> Recently, mental health professionals have begun examining the potential value of religious faith and spirituality.... This study explored the relation between religious faith, spirituality, and mental health outcomes in 236 individuals recovering from substance abuse. We found that recovering individuals tend to report high levels of religious faith and religious affiliation.[19]

Ethic Twenty-Six—An effective corrections ethic must astutely intervene in the recidivistic cycle of addiction and criminality. Laws enacted which criminalize individuals for nonviolent crimes committed as a result of their addiction, fail to address the complexity of human behavior and addiction. The addicted offender is not deterred by harsh sentences and the enactment of such rules and laws; the continued introduction of such is evidence that too many lawmakers either gain political capital from the perception of *get tough on crime* legislative agendas, or fail to comprehend the correlative relationships between addiction and criminality.

As a corrections professional, I witnessed those individuals suffering with addiction matriculate through the courts time after time, and then be sentenced once again to a jail or prison term. The result is disrupted families and broken lives, as well as a fiscal drain on the budgets of local and state government. An intervention model which comprehends the irrationality of this cycle is the concept and implementation of drug courts. As a result of courts

---

19. Pardini, "Religious Faith and Spirituality," 347.

A Theology of Justice

being strained by the growing number of citizens prosecuted for addiction related crimes, the concept of drug courts was introduced to handle nonviolent offenders who presented with a drug- or alcohol-related crime. In an article appearing on the website of the US Department of Justice, Office of Justice Programs, titled "Drug Courts," the concept of drug courts is explained. "Drug courts are specialized court docket programs that target adults charged with or convicted of a crime, youth involved in the juvenile justice system, and parents with pending child welfare cases who have alcohol and other drug dependency problems."[20]

Ethic Twenty-Seven—An effective corrections ethic prioritizes the intervention in the recidivistic cycle of addiction and criminality, through the petitioning for drug courts throughout the country and especially in communities most adversely affected by drug and alcohol addiction.

> Drug courts are usually managed by a nonadversarial and multidisciplinary team including judges, prosecutors, defense attorneys, community corrections, social workers and treatment service professionals. Support from stakeholders representing law enforcement, the family and the community is encouraged through participation in hearings, programming and events like graduation.[21]

The cumulative effect of the concept of morality of association as a positive reinforcement, in treating addiction within communities, will result in the disruption of addiction related maladies, and generationally learned behaviors associated with drinking and drug use. This can facilitate the burgeoning of healthy communities and newly learned lifestyles.

The second environmental factor leading to incarceration is the failure of many offenders to attain a basic high school education. During my tenure at both the Maryland Division of Pretrial Detention and Services, and the Adams County Adult Correctional Complex, the majority of inmates housed at both facilities lacked a high school diploma, or a General Equivalency Diploma. This fact

20. "Drug Courts: Special Feature," para. 1.
21. "Overview of Drug Courts," para. 3.

Environmental Factors Leading to Jail and Prison

is indicative and symptomatic of a population that presented with either, or both, delinquency and truancy during their childhood school years.

For a brief time in 2010, I collaborated with Wordsworth Academy in Harrisburg, Pennsylvania, a special education school or what some refer to as an alternative school. It is possible that experiences at Wordsworth Academy are anomalous; however, the extrapolation of experiences and observations made there may prove instructional in the formation of a corrections ethic. The school accommodated students in elementary school, middle school, and high school. It provided education for students that had been removed from the public school system for disciplinary reasons.

To my expectancy, I found an identical culture to that of the prison system in which I had served for almost two decades. Disappointingly, the argument can be made that the culture at Wordsworth Academy was equally as ominous as either penal institution I had served. In my tenure in corrections I had never been attacked or injured. In a period of approximately two or three months at Wordsworth Academy, I sustained an injury to my head at the hands of a juvenile student, who deliberately and without provocation slammed a classroom door on me during a moment of inattentiveness.

If not disrupted, children's maladaptive behavior and performance in school is a good predictor of future incarceration in jails and prisons in the United States. During my tenure at Wordsworth Academy I was aware with some measure of certainty that a significant number of students would be future inmates, barring significant intervention somewhere during their elementary, middle school, or high school years. To amplify the extent of the crisis, both the Maryland Division of Pretrial Detention and Services and the Adams County Adult Correctional Complex had public schools housed in their respective facilities.

In Maryland the former school at the detention facility provided education for its extensive juvenile population, and was Baltimore City Public School #370. It accommodated grades seventh

A Theology of Justice

through twelfth. In Gettysburg, Pennsylvania, the school at the correctional facility was the Lincoln Intermediate School, and provided education for inmates up until their teen years.

Writing in "New Directions for Youth Development: Deconstructing the School-to-Prison Pipeline," for the US Department of Justice, Office of Justice Programs, Johanna Wald and Daniel J. Olsen make the following observation: "Seventy-five percent of youths under age eighteen who have been sentenced to adult prisons have not passed tenth grade. An estimated 70 percent of the juvenile justice population suffer from learning disabilities, and 33 percent read below the fourth-grade level. The single largest predictor of later arrest among adolescent females is having been suspended, expelled, or held back during the middle school years."[22]

I can recall only two exceptions to this profile of offender in my almost two decades working at the state and county correctional levels. The federal level is more inclined to see a different profile of inmate reflective of white-collar crime. The first exception was an inmate housed at the Baltimore correctional facility who had recently been a student at the prestigious Johns Hopkins University. This inmate, Robert J. Hardwood Jr., worked for me as an inmate office custodian and by all accounts was a brilliant individual. He was incarcerated for the April 1996 killing of fellow alumnus Rex Chao in a campus shooting altercation. The second instance was inmate Kevin Schaefer, who was a student at Gettysburg College and was incarcerated for the April 2009 killing of classmate Emily Silverstein. He, like Robert J. Hardwood Jr., would be confined in my assigned penal institution.

These individuals are the antithesis of inmates filling the jails and prisons in the United States, not only because of their status as well educated, but they also represent offenders who come from socioeconomic backgrounds that are not impoverished. Too often the worst schools are located in communities that suffer from grinding poverty. The conundrum for some scholars and advocates of social justice is whether poor performing schools produce

22. Losen and Wald, *Deconstructing the School-to-Prison Pipeline*, 11.

delinquency, or delinquency contributes to poor performing schools. Perhaps they are coterminous. The formula appears, nevertheless, to include a correlation between poor performing schools, poverty rates, and crime. An article by the United States Government Accountability Office titled "Poverty In America: Consequences for Individuals and the Economy" investigates the question. "Economic Research suggests that individuals living in poverty face an increased risk of adverse outcomes, such as poor health and criminal activity, both of which may lead to reduced participation in the labor market. . . . The economic research we reviewed also points to links between poverty and crime."[23]

Within county jails and state prisons, offenders who originate from advantaged socioeconomic backgrounds and wealth are outliers. While this profile of inmate can be found more readily in the federal prison system, the profile does not reflect the crisis of incarceration relative to poverty, addiction, and underachieving academic performance, that is endemic in the United States with respect to the majority of persons incarcerated today. An effective corrections ethic therefore must implement policies and procedures, standard operating procedures, curricula, and programming which incorporate methodology and mechanisms that comprehend the significance of the morality of authority and the morality of association as environmental determinants upon incarceration trends.

---

23. Nilsen, "Poverty In America," para. 1.

Chapter 6

INDIVIDUAL AGENCY AND INCARCERATION

IN THE PREVIOUS CHAPTER, I have focused on the environmental determinants affecting criminogenic behaviors and tendencies. The fact remains, however, that individuals who have had every advantage socially, socioeconomically, and educationally commit crimes and occupy jails, often leading to federal prisons—which can differ significantly from city and state penal institutions. Crafting a corrections ethic which accounts for maladaptive behavior in the context of individual agency or freewill, juxtaposed with determinism and causativeness, one must consider whether any action is free of external influences.

Individuals lacking the capacity for *moral personality* and *scattered individuals* as John Rawls identifies them in *A Theory of Justice* would seem to describe individuals who intrinsically tend toward criminogenic tendencies, minus the injurious influence of environmental variables. Arguably, this description would seem to suggest influences upon behavior which may be categorized as incorporeal or imperceptible. Hence, people behave badly due to reasons that cannot be measured or are unintelligible by empirical measurements.

Individual Agency and Incarceration

Are individuals capable of heinous crimes simply because they are "bad people," or do "bad people" actually exist, and therefore require no further investigation as to their delinquent behavior? To what extent then does individual agency exist, and to what extent does individual culpability play a role in criminogenic behavior? Patricia E. Erickson and Steven K. Erickson, writing in *Crime, Punishment and Mental Illness: Law and the Behavioral Sciences in Conflict*, make the following observation.

> Criminal law and law generally place great emphasis on the philosophical tradition of moral reasoning as well as on religious ideas concerning good and evil. From these traditions arose the assumption that all people possess free will and that we could and should understand behavior as an outcome of choices persons make as free agents. In contrast, the behavioral sciences that include psychiatry are grounded in a deterministic and empirical tradition and, therefore, examine the causes or reasons for behavior in terms of a person's social, psychological, and biological history and, in addition, in terms of the influence of social structure.[1]

This is in contrast to Rawls introducing the concepts of "unjust," "bad," and "evil." The concept of evil is used in the context of social justice, and in Rawls' definition of good applied to persons in *A Theory of Justice*; however, employment of the word "evil" nevertheless conjures the possibility of existent influences upon behavior, that may extend beyond the scope of social science or criminology. Rawls makes the following assertion. "What moves the evil man is the love of injustice: he delights in the impotence and humiliation of those subject to him and he relishes being recognized by them as the willful author of their degradation."[2]

In the context of corrections ethics, is there any appropriate discussion pertinent to evil as a metaphysical reality, influential in the egregious acts of criminal offenders? The heinous criminal acts of Jeffrey Dahmer, John Wayne Gacy, and Richard Ramirez (known

---

1. Erickson and Erickson, *Crime, Punishment, and Mental Illness*, 10.
2. Rawls, *Theory of Justice*, 386.

as "The Night Stalker") exhaust the capacity of most observers to classify these individuals as simply deranged, and compel some to posit a more malevolent classification of offender. Do offenders in this classification possess redemptive characteristics, or is there no remnant of a rehabilitative constitution?

These individuals could occupy the rare classification of lacking the capacity for moral personality, or scattered individuals. In almost two decades as a director within correctional treatment, I have encountered these individuals in the rarest of occasions. The offenders that are classified in this category are almost nonexistent. Some experts in the discipline of human behavior even go as far as to suggest that given the conditions, all human beings are capable of "evil" behavior, and the potential to behave abhorrently exists within all human capacity. Social psychologist Dr. Philip Zimbardo, professor emeritus at Stanford University, makes this argument regarding human behavior in an article appearing in *Religion Link: Religion Story Ideas & Sources*, titled "The Science of Evil: 'Bad Barrels' or 'Bad Apples'?"

> Zimbardo's book, *The Lucifer-Effect: Understanding How Good People Turn Evil*, draws a compelling parallel between abuse at Abu Ghraib and during the Stanford Prison Experiment, a famous 1971 simulation study headed by Zimbardo that randomly assigned ordinary American college students to portray either guards or prisoners in a mock prison located in a campus building. Within days "guards" began treating "inmates" with sadistic cruelty-much like the abuse visited on the inmates of Abu Ghraib—that forced Zimbardo to end the project, originally planned to run two weeks, a week early. Psychological tests administered before the experiment had revealed no mental problems among the students, nor any differences among those assigned as guards or prisoners. Rather, the situational factors and social dynamics within the fake prison released the capacity for evil inherent in all human beings, leading to behavior

Individual Agency and Incarceration

ordinarily considered abhorrent, Zimbardo said. This, he maintained, also happened at Abu Ghraib.[3]

Ethic Twenty-Eight—An effective corrections ethic must deny the role of evil as a metaphysical reality informing criminogenic behavior. Utilizing the understanding of evil as outlined by Dr. Philip Zimbardo, as existing due to "situation factors and social dynamic," is a more pragmatic approach in interpreting heinous criminal acts. The danger of classifying certain inmate offenders as evil, in a metaphysical construct, is that it disavows the theoretical underpinnings of rehabilitation and treatment.

Ethic Twenty-Nine—An effective corrections ethic must courageously oppose the theoretical premise of capital punishment, although to do so is counterintuitive for many, including this author, and seemingly cathartic for society when considered in the context of the most egregious acts against humanity. The premise of capital punishment suggests that there are certain human beings who are beyond redemption or rehabilitation. While there are offenders who are not within the capacity for rehabilitation to the extent they can live within society, an effective corrections ethic reaffirms the capacity for rehabilitation, to the extent that the vilest offenders are capable of existing within the custody of government-conducted correctional facilities. The right to life for criminals, and law-abiding citizens alike, are *erga omnes* rights and should be considered non-derogable rights.

Arguably, one of the most misunderstood and perplexing of criminogenic behaviors is that of the sex offender. Within the jail and prison culture sex offense crimes are the most taboo. Sex offenders are viewed within correctional settings, by inmates and correctional staff alike, as the least respected of all offenders. It is not unusual for sex offenders to request protective custody during their incarceration period, due to the likelihood of being assaulted by other inmates. As the director of treatment at the Adams County Adult Correctional Complex, one of the challenges faced was the difficulty in having sex offenders attend treatment for two

---

3. "Science of Evil," para. 3.

primary reasons. First, many of the sex offenders did not want to be singled out as such by participating in treatment, which was an acknowledgement of their crime. Second, there were so few practitioners qualified to treat sex offenders.

The consensus when it comes to addressing sex offenders is that this group is highly unpredictable and highly susceptible to reoffending. Whether this position is backed by scientific evidence or tends to be more anecdotal, research is divided on this outcome and often contradicts the accepted beliefs concerning recidivism. Sex offenders represent a group of offenders that are highly scrutinized, with data often presenting varied messages. A 2019 article appearing in *SAGE Journals* titled "On the Effectiveness of Sexual Offender Treatment in Prisons: A Comparison of Two Different Evaluation Designs in Routine Practice" corroborates the complexity of sex-offender treatment. "International meta-analyses on the effects of sex offender treatment revealed that there is considerable variety in the results, and methodological aspects and the context play a significant role."[4]

In an article titled "New Hope for Sex Offender Treatment" by Karen Kersting for the American Psychological Association, the unique challenges presented by this classification of offender is addressed.

> Controversial questions swirl around the correctional system's management of sex offenders: How long should they be incarcerated for their crimes of forcing sex acts on adults or children? How should they be monitored following release? Does psychological treatment in prison actually affect the risk of committing further offenses? And how can courts balance offenders' potential for rehabilitation with a community's need to protect its citizens? Responses to these questions have varied over the years, and, accordingly, so has policy-making by the states and the federal government. Recent policies have been trending toward longer prison sentences and more restrictive after-release monitoring, stemming in part

---

4. Losel et al., "On the Effectiveness," para. 1.

Individual Agency and Incarceration

from a dismal view of treatment programs, treatment advocates say.[5]

To what extent do sex offenders have agency or freewill over their impulses? Do their actions reflect a wanton disregard for law and order, and merit the harshest sentences available to judges, or should sex offenders be treated more along the lines of offenders presenting with addiction, and be treated as having a disorder and sentencing be more inclined toward treatment? One of the challenges relative to how the criminal justice system should respond to sex offenders is determining whether their behavior reflects an innate disorder. If their disorder is innate then sex offenders are as much victims as they are predators. This line of reasoning is rather offensive to many who have been victimized by sex offenders, or are simply advocates for victims of sex offenders.

The question then does not center on the repulsiveness of the crime of sex offenders, for it is one of the most repugnant of all behaviors. The ethical dilemma is, how does the criminal justice system respond to sex offenders: as criminals, or as defective offenders in need of treatment, or perhaps both? To what extent are sex offenders in control of their actions?

Ethic Thirty—An effective corrections ethic reconciles the necessity for the coexistence of both custody and treatment pertaining to the sex offender. The need for strict custodial control is motivated less by the need for punishment, and more by the need for protecting society while simultaneously treating the sex offender.

Due to the particularly revolting nature of this offense, correctional officials need to be vigilant addressing and responding to the offender, while affirming the humanity of the offender and not defining the offender by the crime committed.

Ethic Thirty-One—An effective corrections ethic must be implemented with impartial deliberateness, and avoid the compulsion to respond emotionally. It is improbable that corrections ethics would be adhered to by persons personally affected as victims

---

5. Kersting, "New Hope for Sex Offender Treatment," para. 1.

of crime. If the tenets of corrections ethics are not established with foresight and predetermined prior to established bias, or personal loss as a result of crime, the parameters and intent of a thoughtful corrections ethic may appear untenable.

Many victims of homicidal predators or sex offenders are understandably unable to fully embrace many of the goals of corrections ethics. Even proponents of corrections ethics may be swayed toward punitive correctional practices, if they are unfortunate enough to be victimized in the future. That, however, does not diminish the strength of corrections ethics, as much as it undergirds the fact that corrections ethics should be developed apart from personal bias or investment that individuals may have in a punitive corrections model. Corrections ethics should be conceived behind a *veil of ignorance*. To the extent that no one knows their involvement in the criminal justice system, or when they or their loved ones will be a part of the adjudicatory process, the correctional system vis-à-vis jails and prisons should be envisioned as a fair and impartial system. To put it more succinctly, what would one want jail and prison conditions to be like if one found oneself incarcerated? John Rawls referred to a *just society* as one that is conceived by individuals behind a *veil of ignorance*, unaware of their place within society. Rawls refers to this phenomenon as the *Original Position*, the equivalent of the state of nature for social contract theorists such as Locke, Hobbes, and Rousseau.

> No one knows his place in society, his class position or social status; nor does he know his fortune in the distribution of natural assets and abilities, his intelligence and strength, and the like. Nor, again, does anyone know his conception of the good, the particulars of his rational plan of life, or even the special features of his psychology such as his aversion to risk or liability to optimism or pessimism. More than this, I assume that the parties do not know the particular circumstances of their own society.[6]

---

6. Rawls, *Theory of Justice*, 118.

Individual Agency and Incarceration

For Rawls, the importance of the original position and the veil of ignorance is that individuals would conceive of a just society which positions all men and women with equal opportunities and identical vantage points. The result would be that society then would not possess institutions and societal laws which guaranteed advantages to certain segments of society, while systematically marginalizing segments of the population. Individuals in the original position, behind a veil of ignorance, would seek to achieve what Rawls calls *Maximin*, in the event that anyone would discover themselves in the least desired position in society. Maximin is the concept that those in the original position create an environment that gives to the most vulnerable in society the smallest deficit imaginable.

Rawls explains the concept of Maximin. "This is evident from the fact that the two principles are those a person would choose for the design of a society in which his enemy is to assign him his place. The Maximin rule tells us to rank alternatives by their worst possible outcomes: we are to adopt the alternative the worst outcome of which is superior to the worst outcomes of the others."[7]

Ethic Thirty-Two—An effective corrections ethic must be conceived by those in the original position behind a veil of ignorance. Although by necessity jails and prisons must exist, the architects of treatment and rehabilitation, corrections officials, courts and judges, and societal attitudes should envision or conceptualize jails and prisons with the Maximin as the guiding principle.

In the context of corrections, the original position should consist of those who do not profit from the proliferation of jails and prisons, such as correctional entrepreneurial-privatization corporations, elected officials, contractual vendors such as medical providers, telecommunications networks, refectory suppliers of inmate commissary accounts and meals, all of which have an invested interest in the proliferation and human stocking of jails and prisons. The primary architects within the original position should be individuals and organizations, comprised of independent entities, or entities with similar constitutions and goals.

---

7. Rawls, *Theory of Justice*, 132–33.

A Theology of Justice

Some examples are the Pennsylvania Prison Society, Amnesty International USA, Solitary Watch, Prison Watch Network, ACLU National Prison Project, and the United Nations Standard Minimum Rules for the Treatment of Prisoners.

The final category of offenders, in the context of individual agency and incarceration to be considered in this corrections ethic, is the seriously mentally ill offender. Unfortunately, jails and prisons in the United States have become filled with mentally ill offenders, due to a process known as deinstitutionalization. A 2020 article published by *Mental Health America* titled "The Legacy Of Deinstitutionalization" describes the purpose of such.

> In today's "deinstitutionalized" world, prisons and jails function as makeshift asylums with the shared goal of containing and segregating Black and Brown disabled communities from the rest of society. As of 2014, approximately 356,000 incarcerated people have severe mental illness, 10 times the number of people with severe mental illness in state hospitals.[8]

Over the last four decades as mental health facilities were closed, and mentally ill patients were transitioned to outpatient clinics in the community, many patients were unsuccessful in maintaining the regimen of treatment required to successfully reintegrate back into the community. The *Encyclopedia of Mental Disorders* describes yet another aspect of deinstitutionalization.

> Deinstitutionalization is a long-term trend wherein fewer people reside as patients in mental hospitals and fewer mental health treatments are delivered in public hospitals. This trend is directly due to the process of closing public hospitals and the ensuing transfers of patients to community-based mental health services in the late twentieth century. It represents the dissipation of patients over a wider variety of health care settings and geographic areas.[9]

---

8. Nishar, "Legacy of Deinstitutionalization," para.1.
9. Polgar, "Deinstitutionalization," para. 1.

Individual Agency and Incarceration

As a result, there was a proliferation of the homeless population throughout the United States that presented with mental illnesses. Tragically, many of the mentally ill deinstitutionalized during the same period, began to populate jails and prisons around the country. This phenomenon evolved into what is now a national epidemic of jails and prisons serving as de facto psychiatric hospitals. A 2006 Justice Department survey—in an article written by Erik Eckholm, titled "Inmates Report Mental Illness at High Levels"—demonstrates the duration of this problem over the last couple of decades.

> The findings underscore what every prison administrator knows-that large numbers of individuals with mental health problems are cycling through their facilities.... Prisoners with mental health problems were more likely to have had repeated incarcerations and substance abuse problems and to have been homeless.... One in three state prisoners, one in four federal prisoners and one in six jail prisoners had received some form of mental health treatment, often medication.[10]

The process of transcarceration, or transitioning mentally ill individuals from psychiatric hospitals to jails and prisons, has exasperated an already overwhelmed penal system. As a director at both the Maryland Division of Pretrial Detention and Services, and the Adams County Adult Correctional Complex, I witnessed correctional staff vis-à-vis correctional officers ill-prepared for the day-to-day confinement of mentally ill inmates. Too often, correctional officers interpreted the behaviors of mentally ill inmates, as an affront to their authority or deliberate recalcitrance.

As a result, the mentally ill who fill the jails and prisons in the United States are particularly vulnerable to abuse by correctional officials. One form of abuse is increased sentences of inmates due to their failure to follow jail and prison rules and regulations. An inmate can extend his or her jail or prison sentence if he or she is found guilty of infractions by jail or prison disciplinary hearing boards. At the Adams County Adult Correctional Complex, the

---

10. Eckholm, "Inmates Report Mental Illness," para. 4.

A Theology of Justice

disciplinary hearing board consisted of an administrative assistant and security personnel, possessing no training in mental health and often no training beyond high school.

The result would more often than not be that the inmate was found guilty and placed into solitary confinement or *the hole* in jail and prison parlance. Many seriously mentally ill offenders experience decompensation or deterioration of their mental health due to the less-than-therapeutic environment of jails and prisons. This is made worse, however, when mentally ill offenders are placed in extreme conditions such as solitary confinement.

Solitary confinement restricts the offender's human interaction and stimuli by placing them in cells with no windows for twenty-three hours per day. The restriction to solitary confinement often has devastating results for offenders in general, and exponentially so for the seriously mentally ill inmate.

In the *Journal of the American Academy of Psychiatry and the Law Online*, an article titled "Solitary Confinement and Mental Illness in U.S. Prisons: A Challenge for Medical Ethics," written by Jeffrey L. Metzner, MD, and Jamie Fellner, Esq., cites the challenges of solitary confinement.

> In recent years, physicians have increasingly confronted a new challenge: the prolonged solitary confinement of prisoners with serious mental illness, a corrections practice that has become prevalent despite the psychological harm it can cause. There has been scant professional or academic attention to the unique ethics-related quandary of physicians and other healthcare professionals when prisons isolate inmates with mental illness. . . . Solitary confinement is recognized as difficult to withstand; indeed, psychological stressors such as isolation can be as clinically distressing as physical torture. Nevertheless, U.S. prison officials have increasingly embraced a variant of solitary confinement to punish and control difficult or dangerous prisoners.[11]

---

11. Metzner and Fellner, "Solitary Confinement and Mental Illness," 104.

Individual Agency and Incarceration

Ethic Thirty-Three—An effective corrections ethic emphasizes the lack of agency or freewill among the seriously mentally ill offenders in jails and prisons when lacking proper treatment measures. When offenders present with serious mental illness, they are clearly acting as those lacking the capacity for moral personality.

Jail and prison policies and procedures, standard operating procedures, and mechanisms must require that all punitive measures against the seriously mentally ill offender be in consultation with institutional mental health providers. Wardens, commissioners, and correctional officials must be required to document and make available for public review confinement decisions affecting mentally ill offenders.

Chapter 7

TREATMENT VERSUS SECURITY

ALTERNATIVES TO JAIL AND PRISON

A SIGNIFICANT ARGUMENT CAN be made for the assertion that within the culture of jails and prisons in the United States, the single most adversarial relationship is between treatment staff and security or custodial personnel. The reasons for the contentious nature of the relationship can be attributed to several variables. One significant reason is that at the county and state level, treatment staff represent the professional hiring classification of jails and prisons. Many of the positions within treatment require at minimum a college degree and in some instances a master's degree. The most highly specialized positions within treatment require an earned doctorate.

On the security side of the house, as it is often referred to, there is reliance more upon systems of tenure or "coming up through the ranks." It is not unusual for correctional officers to enter the correctional profession directly from high school, and rise through the ranks over a twenty-year period to become a warden or the senior facility administrator.

Immediately, there exists the potential for an adversarial relationship predicated upon differing worldviews, and the

Treatment versus Security

interpretation of phenomena within corrections from a wide conceptual chasm. Many departments of correction have begun to require higher-ranking corrections officials, such as majors and wardens, to possess at minimum a bachelor's degree. The caveat, however, and the loophole is that many department of corrections, still allow for experience to be counted in lieu of a college education.

Therefore, it is not unusual to have a scenario such as I had at the Adams County Adult Correctional Complex, whereby the warden of a correctional facility, having a high school diploma, was supervising individuals with college and graduate degrees. The challenge is that often these individuals have not "done the work" of thinking through the science of corrections, the sociological and or anthropological constructs, antecedent to "presenting problems" within the corrections environment.

At the county and state level there exists a quasi-class division between treatment and security. At times the tension between the two is palpable. Too often, the theoretical divide between security and treatment arises from different perspectives relative to the inmate population.

Generally speaking, correctional officers and inmates have an antagonistic relationship often bordering on disdain. The confrontational interactions experienced by security personnel, at the line-officer level during the early stages of their career, are often internalized and become the reference point of the custodial chain of command throughout the tenure of the officer and even the warden.

Conversely, treatment professionals suffer from the perception of being naïve concerning the inmate in particular, and security measures in general. Like many perceptions there is some justification for this opinion. Initially treatment personnel have less experience and training in security, contraband, inmate manipulation, policies and procedures, and understanding of the operations within the correctional facility. Fortunately, most jails and prisons now require all employees to either attend their training academy or successfully complete an initial orientation training, prior to working inside of the facility.

After almost two decades inside of correctional settings, I understood most, if not all, of the characteristics of the day-to-day security operations. It takes time to understand the profession of corrections. The culture of corrections is a very complicated and dynamic environment, and it takes many years to understand its various nuances. Failure to understand this environment can and will result in loss of life, and or careers. I have witnessed an inmate manipulate a doctor into aiding his escape from the correctional facility in Maryland. I have witnessed an inmate manipulate a treatment specialist romantically in Gettysburg. The setting is rife with opportunities for failure.

Beyond these differences, however, is the very fundamental difference in the conceptualization of the individual self-worth of each inmate, by security and treatment personnel. The antithesis in conceptualization by security and treatment is embodied in the dichotomy earlier referenced, in the juxtaposition of the social contract theorist Thomas Hobbes, in contrast with John Locke, Jean-Jacques Rousseau, and John Rawls. As we recall, for Thomas Hobbes the state of nature for humanity is dystopian:

> No Arts; no Letters; no society; and which is worst of all, continual *feare*, and danger of violent death; And life of man, solitary, *poore*, nasty, brutish, and short. It may seem strange to some man, that has not well weighed these things; that Nature should thus dissociate, and render men apt to invade, and destroy one another.[1]

Heretofore, this corrections ethic has developed the aspects of social contract theory emanating from Locke, Rousseau, and Rawls. This chapter will concern itself with the culture of corrections more reflective of Thomas Hobbes's observation of humanity. Unfortunately, many jail and prison environments, through neglect and indifference, have experienced a regression of humanity's state of nature to reflect an artificial Hobbesian condition.

---

1. Hobbes, *Leviathan*, 62.

Treatment versus Security

In confinement, the epitome of the "nasty, brutish, and poor" conditions or state of nature defined by Hobbes is the victimization of inmates by predatory inmates through jail and prison rape. The crisis of rape in jails and prisons had become so critical that in 2003 then-President George W. Bush enacted the "Prison Rape Elimination Act" in an effort to address this human rights violation. Jail and prison rape is an act of power, in which inmates use coerced sex to establish the rank or dominance of inmate authority. In addition to the physical and psychological injuries incurred during a jail or prison rape, the spread of HIV and AIDS is an ever-present reality for many inmates.

Writing in *Prison Conditions: Overcrowding, Disease, Violence, And Abuse*, Roger Smith, in consultation with the John Jay College of Criminal Justice, chronicled the epidemic.

> Prison rape is an unpleasant subject that many in society choose to ignore. According to Lara Stemple, executive director of Stop Prison Rape (SPR), prison rape is an institutionalized atrocity that goes against a person's most basic human rights, causes the spread of disease, and creates a violent cycle both inside and outside prison walls. A recent study done of four Midwestern state prisons reported that one in five male prisoners reported a forced or pressured sexual experience while in prison. According to a 2001 Human Rights Watch report, anywhere from 200,000 to 650,000 inmates (mostly males) are raped in the United States every year.[2]

Having worked in the correctional setting for almost two decades, I can declare emphatically that jail and prison rape is a breach of security, a consequence of correctional personnel failing to maintain custody and control of inmate movement in the facility. Correctional staff pride themselves in maintaining control of the correctional institution, and maintaining inmate accountability at all times. The location of an inmate should always be known by jail and prison correctional officers, or civilian staffers if attending classes or if present in the clinic or hospital. Strict accountability

---

2. Smith, *Prison Conditions*, 74.

of inmate movement and location would almost eliminate jail and prison rape. This is a fact.

Jail and prison rapes occur for at least two reasons. First, there has come to be a general acceptance of rape almost as a reality of jail and prison culture. The rape of an inmate seems to be almost a rite of passage in some correctional institutions. Second, correctional officers use rape as a method of control over the inmate population. This is done by allowing a vulnerable inmate to be placed in a setting or circumstances, which would easily facilitate the victimization of a weaker inmate by a predatory inmate. This is done by looking the other way during a rape, or failing to bring a predatory inmate "up on charges" for rape. It creates an environment of indifference, and forces inmates to create their own security systems through gangs, or protective inmates, to whom they commit themselves to sexually for protection.

Ethic Thirty-Four—An effective corrections ethic advocates for enforcing punitive measures on not only predatory inmates, but also on correctional officers and institutional staff who fail to protect inmates and report jail and prison rape. A jail or prison, and correctional officials complicit in the culture of jail or prison rape, must be held liable for criminal prosecution in a court of law. Correction officials should not have immunity from criminal prosecution in the case of jail and prison rape. Jail and prison rape is preventable.

The violence associated with jail and prison rape must be viewed not only as a human rights concern, but also must be addressed as a health crisis as well. The spread of HIV and AIDS is not only a threat to the jail and prison population, but also the community as inmates transition to ex-offender status. An article from *NBC News* titled "Condoms Urged in Prisons to Curb AIDS: Black Leaders Call for Steps to Slow HIV's Spread in Minority Population" captures this crisis:

> U.S. prisons should make condoms available to inmates and test for HIV as part of a broader effort to curb the spread of AIDS among blacks, hit disproportionately hard by the incurable disease. . . .

Treatment versus Security

Condoms are banned or unavailable in 95 percent of U.S. prisons. It said state prisons in Mississippi and Vermont make condoms available, as do county jails in New York City, Philadelphia, Washington, D.C., San Francisco and Los Angeles.

"HIV transmission does indeed occur in prison," said the report's author, Robert Fullilove, professor of clinical sociomedical sciences at Columbia University in New York.[3]

Given the artificial state of nature of jails and prisons, "nasty, brutish, and poor," an effective corrections ethic interprets the call for condom access in jails and prisons as a necessary discussion, in order to slow the spread of HIV and AIDS among the inmate population and their respective family members upon their release from incarceration. The advocacy by certain organizations for condom access by inmates, is consistent with the repudiation of jail and prison rape. However, my position-my stance stops short of including condom access in jails and prisons as an effective corrections ethic, due to the sensibilities of both religious and civic groups ardently committed to the cause of prison reform, yet opposed to consensual sexual contact among the inmate population.

Throughout the United States jails and prisons are sites of suicides, homicides, and deaths from causes that are classified as more or less ambiguous medical reasons. Medical malpractice within jails and prisons is a serious problem that too often goes uninvestigated. As a director within both the Maryland Division of Pretrial Detention and Services, and the Adams County Adult Correctional Complex, I recall attending administrator meetings of which I was often a board member, hearing contractual medical providers routinely being asked to explain why "inmate medical requests" were either not being answered, or why there was consistent dereliction responding to inmate medical requests in a timely manner.

Often, extensive justifications for not seeing inmates were framed in the context of incompetent request slip processing, or

---

3. "Condoms Urged in Prisons," paras. 1, 10–11.

procedural wrangling over how the request order was filled out or placed in the inmate medical request box. This discussion and similar untenable justifications for inmates not being seen by medical providers in a timely fashion went on for years and was a consistent challenge for jail and prison medical providers and corrections administrators.

In the Maryland facility where I served for fifteen years, the medical contractors consistently failed audits and inspections. It was almost assured that the medical provider would be the reason the Maryland Division of Pretrial Detention and Services failed the audit as an organization. In my fifteen-year tenure the changing of medical contractors was more or less a bi-annual occurrence. In an article for the American Civil Liberties Union titled "Federal Judge Approves ACLU Settlement Forcing Sweeping Improvements In Conditions At Baltimore City Jail," a news release cites the following.

> The jail has been riddled with problems for years resulting from the failure of jail officials to provide necessary medical treatment. Detainees with uncontrolled and untreated diabetes have died, a detainee with a history of cancer went three months without having a suspicious lump in her breast diagnosed and detainees have gone months without receiving needed medications upon entering the jail. A 2008 Department of Justice (DOJ) report found that less than half of requests for medical care were responded to in a timely manner and concluded that healthcare in the jail is compromised by poor administrative and nursing systems.[4]

The prevailing attitude of the correctional staff at the Maryland facility, security and treatment alike was that the inmate population was primarily an indigent population, and therefore should not complain about substandard medical provisions. The insistence that the poor medical service which they received was the best medical attention most had ever experienced outside of the

---

4. "Federal Judge Approves ACLU Settlement," para. 9.

Treatment versus Security

jail and should suffice-was a pervasive attitude throughout, and one that came to seem like a tenable argument at the time.

Tragically, the medical malpractice witnessed in the Maryland facility is not an isolated occurrence, but is a part of the larger medical culture within jails and prisons throughout the United States. The Wheeler Correctional Facility located in Georgia, and overseen by the Corrections Corporation of America, now CoreCivic, serves to further demonstrate this. In an article written by Bruce A. Dixon for *Black Agenda Report*, titled "Medical Neglect Stalks Georgia Prisons," prisoner medical neglect is documented in the case of inmate Arnold Porter.

> According to a complaint filed in US District Court in Dublin Ga, Porter repeatedly and insistently sought medical aid . . . informing Dr. Sightler, and a prison nurse of his symptoms . . . chest pain, shortness of breath, profuse sweating and the other classic markers of cardiac disease . . . but the first appointment with Dr. Sightler was delayed a full 35 days.[5]

Cases of medical neglect within jails and prisons are not outliers, but rather speak to a widespread culture of correctional medical malfeasance. A 2021 report titled "Disgraced Doctors, Unlicensed Officials: Prisons Face Criticism over Health Care" illuminates this epidemic. Written by Keri Blakinger for *The Marshall Project*,

> The nonprofit National Commission on Correctional Health Care has urged since 1999 that jail and prison medical staff members have the same credentials as those who work outside, in settings like hospitals. But states often allow medical staffers in correctional facilities to work under licenses that are restricted because of past disciplinary issues.[6]

John Rawls included in the category of primary goods that of *health and vigor* in what Rawls referred to as "natural primary

---

5. Dixon, "Medical Neglect Stalks Georgia Prisons," para. 3.
6. Blakinger, "Disgraced Doctors," para. 12.

goods." Rawls also defined self-respect as the most important of all primary goods. The jail and prison conditions in the United States relative to medical malpractice negate or take away optimum opportunity for health and vigor, as well as the self respect of inmates incarcerated within their institutions.

The loss of health and vigor and self respect leaves many inmates with a sense of hopelessness and despair. The conditions of poor healthcare, overcrowding, rape, disease, violence, shame, and isolation are often direct contributing factors to inmate suicide in jails and prisons. Rawls defines self-respect in this way

> I have mentioned that perhaps the most important primary good is that of self-respect. . . . We may define self-respect (or self-esteem) as having two aspects. First of all, as we noted earlier, it includes a person's sense of his own value, his secure conviction that his conception of his good, his plan of life, is worth carrying out. And second, self-respect implies a confidence in one's ability, so far as it is within one's power, to fulfill one's intentions.[7]

Ethic Thirty-Five—An effective corrections ethic requires jails and prisons to make transparent their policies and procedures, standard operating procedures, mechanisms, and inmate medical requests, relative to the medical facilities and clinics operating within correctional facilities. This includes oversight by outside regulatory or oversight committees composed of medical professionals, medical ethicists, and concerned citizen groups. A contributing factor of medical malpractice in correctional medical facilities and clinics is their ability to operate clandestinely. Transparency within medical facilities and clinics facilitates the "health and vigor," and the "self-respect" of the inmate population.

The treatment versus security or custody divide is evident in the characterization of jail and prison conditions by treatment staff juxtaposed with security custodians. A survey of security staff may find conditions within jail and prisons described as less than urgent, and the security staff may not be persuaded that in fact there is a crisis the magnitude of which requires a major overhaul

7. Rawls, *Theory of Justice*, 386.

Treatment versus Security

of the jail and prison system. The treatment or non-uniformed personnel would tend to focus on the issues of rape, violence, suicide, medical malpractice, and other challenges as emblematic of the treatment versus custody or security tension, and interpretation of the state of jails and prisons.

Lorna A. Rhodes captures the tension writing in *Total Confinement: Madness and Reason in the Maximum Security Prison*:

> For both custody and treatment workers it is axiomatic that friction between them results from their differential possession of power and knowledge. . . . Sharing historical roots and a fundamentally similar method for locating individuals in institutional space, custody and treatment are united in mutual dependence. But this very interdependence also positions custody and treatment workers as one another's most vigorous critics.[8]

The polarization between security and treatment is cause for great concern and should be a focus of corrections ethics. The relationship can border on extreme animosity at times.

The first time I witnessed the immediate aftermath of an inmate suicide was in my capacity as a director at the Maryland Division of Pretrial Detention and Services. The scene was the Women's Detention Center, or the WDC. A young female hanged herself and lay motionless on the jail floor. The image is forever etched in my mind of a young woman lifeless, the dried regurgitation spewed from her mouth onto her face. Suicide in jails and prisons is a consistent challenge for correctional facilities. Inmates who are at high risk of either suicide or attempting suicide are offenders who are being incarcerated in local jails and prisons for the first time, especially during the intake process; inmates who are mentally ill; and individuals from the community who once were highly respected or held positions of authority in community.

Police officers, former correctional officers, and uniformed personnel once representing the corrections profession are especially vulnerable to suicide or attempted suicide. All high risk offenders in jails and prisons are normally evaluated and placed

---

8. Rhodes, *Total Confinement*, 133–34.

A Theology of Justice

on suicide watch. During my tenure at the Maryland correctional facility, there were several occasions when former correctional officers and one former police officer occupied what was known as "R" section or protective custody. Tragically, at least one of the officers committed suicide.

Offenders, who once occupied significant stations within society and fall from grace, experience what John Rawls refers to as *moral shame*.

> Thus someone is liable to moral shame when he prizes as excellences of his person those virtues that his plan of life requires and is framed to encourage. He regards the virtues . . . as properties that his associates want in him and that he wants in himself. . . . Actions and traits that manifest or betray the absence of these attributes in his person are likely then to occasion shame, and so is the awareness or recollection of these defects.[9]

Although some suicides in jails and prisons cannot be averted, most suicides are preventable. Correctional officers and treatment staff should be trained to recognize the warning signs of inmates who are suicidal, and all attempts, no matter how feeble, must be taken seriously and documented. Suicides then are for the most part a breach of security. Correctional officers are expected to "do rounds" at regular intervals to prevent suicides from occurring. When inmates are on "suicide watch" and still commit suicide, there is a failure in the fidelity of both correctional officers and treatment personnel to perform their duties professionally.

Ethic Thirty-Six—An effective corrections ethic affirms that security personnel and treatment staff are equally responsible for jail and prison conditions, which minimize the possibility of inmate suicide. Policies and procedures, standard operating procedures, inmate handbooks, mechanisms, and annual training of correctional employees must ensure that both security and treatment personnel are properly trained to recognize the warning signs of suicidal inmates. Correctional employees charged with safeguarding vulnerable or at-risk inmates who commit suicide

---

9. Rawls, *Theory of Justice*, 390.

Treatment versus Security

must be subject to a full review of job performance to evaluate adherence to, or noncompliance with, suicide risk-management procedures.

Finally, two classifications of offenders who pose significant challenges for jail and prison treatment and security personnel are female and juvenile offenders. Too often, this classification of offender is incarcerated within the rubric of a general corrections philosophy, without attention to the unique needs of each. Female and juvenile offenders are required to be segregated from the adult male population within jails and prisons at all times. Female and juvenile offenders should not be within proximity to adult male offenders during their incarceration period. The rare occasion may be to allow for adult male and adult female offenders to attend special events while supervised by correctional officers, or in the context of supervised group treatment sessions.

Jails and prisons must make special provisions for female inmates, relative to unique gender concerns to ensure their health and welfare during incarceration. Modern criminology advances the idea that even the physical structures of jail and prison annexes housing female inmates be constructed with the psychological profile of female inmates in mind. This is particularly critical when the number of female inmates serving time in jail and prison has exponentially increased. A 2020 publication by the Sentencing Project titled "Incarcerated Women and Girls" illuminates this growing trend.

> Over the past quarter century, there has been a profound change in the involvement of women within the criminal justice system. This is the result of more expansive law enforcement efforts, stiffer drug sentencing laws, and post-conviction barriers to reentry that uniquely affect women. The female incarcerated population stands over seven times higher than in 1980. More than 60% of women in state prisons have a child under the age of 18.[10]

While this upsurge has occurred for females incarcerated in jails and prisons, the incarceration of juvenile offenders has

10. "Incarcerated Women and Girls," para. 1.

A Theology of Justice

undergone a significant philosophical change as well, leading to an increase of juveniles in jails and prisons. A study conducted by the Juvenile Law Center titled "Children in Prison" addresses the problem.

> Tens of thousands of children are incarcerated in youth prisons every day; thousands more are also locked up in adult prisons and jails.... Many youth prisons are called "schools," but few of these facilities provide either quality education services children need to heal. Too many incarcerated youth are subject to solitary confinement-often for 22–24 hours per day-strip searches, shackles, and chemical sprays.[11]

The correctional system comprised of jails and prisons in the United States faces a formidable task in housing offenders that present with complex challenges and needs. It is essential that security and treatment professionals comprehend the need for the specialized treatment each respective group requires. The majority of inmates will be reintegrated into society at some juncture of his or her life. Treatment, security, and society would do well to understand their humane treatment as an investment in the communities we all share and are affected by.

Those in the original position, behind a veil of ignorance, envisioning and conceptualizing a state of nature more reflective of John Locke, Jean-Jacques Rousseau, and John Rawls, could conceivably establish a society where jails and prisons either do not exist due to the principles of justice, or their use is employed minimally as a last resort. The concept of jails and prisons would be foreign to the initial comprehension of individuals in such a state. Presently, jails and prisons are part of the initial conceptualization of many individuals in the United States, relative to responding to crime and criminogenic behavior. Incarceration is part of the American psyche.

The goal of this corrections ethic is to engage both casual observer, criminal justice expert, jurist, activist, theologian, and human rights advocate in a paradigm shift away from jails and

11. "Children in Prison," paras. 1–2.

Treatment versus Security

prisons, to conceptualizing alternatives to incarceration, or more specifically to imagine alternative sentencing.

In an article titled "Reinventing Community Corrections," appearing in *The University of Chicago Press Journals*, Francis T. Cullen, Cheryl Lero Johnson, and Daniel P. Mears address the potential and challenges of alternative sentencing.

> Community corrections in the twenty-first century faces three challenges: how to be an alternative to imprisonment, how to be a conduit for reducing recidivism, and how to do less harm to offenders and their families and communities. Community corrections will reduce imprisonment only if its use is viewed as a legitimate form of punishment and is incentivized, which involves subsidizing the use of community sanctions and making communities pay to imprison offenders (e.g., a cap-and-trade system). To reduce recidivism, it will be necessary to hold officials accountable for this outcome, to ensure that evidence-based supervision is practiced, to use technology to deliver treatment services, and to create information systems that can guide the development, monitoring, and evaluation of interventions. Doing less harm—avoiding iatrogenic effects—will require nonintervention with low-risk offenders, reducing the imposition of needless constraints on offenders (i.e., collateral consequences), and creating opportunities for offenders to be redeemed.[12]

Ethic Thirty-Seven—An effective corrections ethic requires civic organizations, religious organizations, and nonprofit organizations within the community—in solidarity—to eradicate the widespread use of jails and prisons, through due diligence in educating themselves on the available alternatives to jail and prison. The Black Church in particular, so dramatically impacted by jails and prisons, is recommended to create within its organization an Alternative Sentencing Commission or auxiliary, as part of its programming. For our purposes, I will refer to this as the Paul and

---

12. Cullen et al., "Reinventing Community Corrections," para. 1.

A Theology of Justice

Silas Alternative Sentencing Initiative, or PASASI. These alternative sentencing options are provided here.

I. Drug Courts as an alternative to incarceration.

II. Diversion Programs as an alternative to incarceration.

III. Deferred Sentencing Programs as an alternative to incarceration.

IV. Restorative Justice as an alternative to incarceration.

V. Home Detention as an alternative to incarceration.

VI. Weekend Jail Program as an alternative to incarceration.

VII. Work Release Program during incarceration to maintain employment and housing.

VIII. Community Service Program as an alternative to incarceration.

IX. Electronic Monitoring Program as an alternative to incarceration.

X. Sober Living Environment Program as an alternative to incarceration.

XI. Day Reporting Center Program as an alternative to incarceration.

XII. Intensive Probation Supervision (IPS) Program as an alternative to incarceration.

Alternative sentencing is the most effective method for stemming the proliferation of jails and prisons in the United States. While it does not serve as a panacea for the problem of incarceration of citizens, it represents a major shift in ideology relative to incarceration.

Ethic Thirty-Eight—An effective corrections ethic, as a final alternative sentencing mechanism, has at its disposal the use of the *Individual's Right to Petition* the United Nations for redress of human rights violations. W. E. B. Du Bois in conjunction with the NAACP made use of this mechanism in October of 1947, in order to bring attention to the violations of *negroes'* human rights in the United States by the United States government.

In an article titled "W.E.B. Du Bois's Historic U.N. Petition Continues to Inspire Human Rights Advocacy," by Jamil Dakwar, this watershed moment is retold.

> Seventy years ago this week, the oldest civil rights organization in the world, the NAACP, submitted a petition to the newly established United Nations demanding accountability for human rights violations against African Americans in the United States. The 96 page petition was written over the course of a year under the editorial supervision of W.E.B. Du Bois. Its six chapters, each written by a leading expert, cover topics ranging from slavery and Jim Crow to voting rights, criminal justice, education, employment and access to health care-areas in which discrimination remains deeply rooted to this day.[13]

It is imperative that persons of color consider the Individual's Right To Petition the United Nations, as a mechanism for redress of human rights violations resulting from jail and prison abuses. With the politicization and ever increasing partisanship of our judicial system, marginalized communities have an alternative means to pursue justice—the individual's right to petition the United Nations, specifically the Office of the United Nations High Commissioner for Human Rights—OHCHR "Complaints Procedures."

The existence and proliferation of jails and prisons, as well as the staggering number of Americans incarcerated, is an indictment of the United States in a variety of ways. First, the thousands of people incarcerated each year in the United States requires a discussion relative to the systems which make up the very essence of American society. Inconvenient questions probe the inability of so many to successfully live within a society freely. Do the structures of American society create a social vortex, which siphon a certain portion of its citizens into a ghettoized dispensable population,

---

13. Dakwar, "W.E.B. Du Bois's Historic U.N. Petition," para. 1.

and is this phenomenon or dispensable portion of society necessary to power the engines of American economics, therefore being a necessary evil within such a state as ours?

Or, is the social vortex siphon less insidious and does it reflect the result of the "perfect storm" of circumstances which marginalize individuals and entire communities? Second, the proliferation of jails and prisons in the United States reflects a failure within our culture to invest in and develop an intentionally segmented portion of society. Jails and prisons represent a waste of human talent. Jails and prisons are the repository for neglected and culturally atrophied individuals, groups, and communities. The existence of jails and prisons is reliant upon inadequate housing, nonexistent prenatal care, lack of comprehensive healthcare from infancy throughout adulthood, inadequate school systems, lack of economic development and employment, and non-assurance of safe and secure neighborhoods. All of these variables are seemingly unrelated and noncontiguous; however, they have a very deterministic role in the proliferation of jail and prison populations.

Finally, this book began with a vigorous repudiation of Angela Davis's work and book *Are Prisons Obsolete?* After many chapters, research, and working through my ideas in a systematic methodology, my repudiation of a conceptualized society without jails and prisons has been challenged. With a paradigm shift, a "move," from the conceptualization of jails and prisons to alternative sentencing, I can visualize a societal landscape free of jails and prisons and not feel utopian in my conclusions. This reality is far removed from the second decade of the twenty-first century, but it is attainable. Whether or not it will be attained is a very different discussion.

The lingering question, pertinent to the elimination of jails and prisons in the future, will be the remaining dilemma of accounting for those Rawls referred to as incapable of achieving the capacity for moral personality, who are those scattered individuals within our society, who represent a small portion of the jail and prison population. Perhaps the next author of a corrections ethic will resolve the last remaining justification for jails and prisons within our society.

Bibliography

Adams, Chris. "Race and the Criminalization of Drugs." *National Press Foundation*, April 22, 2021. https://nationalpress.org/topic/race-and-the-criminalization-of-drugs/.

Aucoin, Brent. Review of *Down on Parchman Farm: The Great Prison in the Mississippi Delta* by William Banks Taylor. *H-Net Reviews* (2001). https://www.h-net.org/reviews/showpdf.php?id=4808.

Barth, Karl. *The Christian Community and the Civil Community, Community, State, and Church: Three Essays.* New York: Anchor, 1960.

Bell, Carl C. "DSM-IV: Diagnostic and Statistical Manual of Mental Disorders." *JAMA* 272.10 (1994) 828–29.

Bertram, Christopher. "Jean Jacques Rousseau." In *The Stanford Encyclopedia of Philosophy* (Winter 2020 Edition), edited by Edward N. Salta, n.p. https://plato.stanford.edu/archives/win2020/entries/rousseau/.

Bivens, Donna, et al. "Flipping the Script: White Privilege and Community Building." http://www.capd.org/white-privilege.

Blakinger, Keri. "Disgraced Doctors, Unlicensed Officials: Prisons Face Criticism over Health Care." *NBC News*, July 1, 2021. https://www.nbcnews.com/news/us-news/disgraced-doctors-unlicensed-officials-prisons-face-criticism-over-health-care-n1272743.

Blitzman, Jay. "Shutting Down the School-to-Prison Pipeline." *American Bar Association* 47.1 (2021) 20–22.

Cavanaugh, Maureen. "The African-American Railroad Experience." *KPBS*, March 23, 2010. https://www.kpbs.org/news/living/2010/03/23/african-american-railroad-experience.

"Children In Prison." https://jlc.org/children-prison.

Coles, Roberta L., and Charles Green. *The Myth of the Missing Black Father.* New York: Columbia University Press, 2009.

"Condoms Urged in Prisons to Curb AIDS." *NBC News*, November 16, 2006. https://www.nbcnews.com/I'd/wbna15753803.

Cosden, Darrell. *A Theology of Work: Work in the New Creation.* Eugene, OR: Wipf & Stock, 2006.

Bibliography

Covin, Larry Donell, Jr. "Homelessness, Poverty, and Incarceration: The Criminalization of Despair." *Journal of Forensic Psychology Research and Practice* 12.5 (2012) 439–56.

———. *Thirteen Turns: A Theology Resurrected From the Gallows of Jim Crow Christianity*. Eugene, OR: Wipf & Stock, 2020.

Cudd, Ann, and Seena Eftekhari. "Contractarianism." In *The Stanford Encyclopedia of Philosophy* (Winter 2021 Edition), edited by Edward N. Zalta, n.p. https://plato.stanford.edu/archives/win2021/entries/contractarianism/.

Cullen, Francis T., et al. "Reinventing Community Corrections." *Crime and Justice* 46.1 (2017) 27–93.

Dakwar, Jamil. "W.E.B. DuBois's Historic U.N. Petition Continues to Inspire Human Rights Advocacy." *American Civil Liberties Union* (blog), October 25, 2017. https://www.aclu.org/blog/human-rights/human-rights-and-racial-justice/web-du-boiss-historic-un-petition-continues.

Day, Dorothy. *On Poverty.* https://www.catholicworker.org/dorothyday/themes/On%20Poverty%20(Dorothy%20Day).pdf.

Dennis, Andrea L. "The Music of Mass Incarceration." *Landslide*, November/December 2020. https://www.americanbar.org/groups/intellectual_property_law/publications/landslide/2020-21/november-december/music-mass-incarceration/.

Dhingra, Neil. "Karl Barth Visits Three Prisons." *Covenant*, May 27, 2016. https://covenant.livingchurch.org/2016/05/2/7/karl-barth-visits-three-prisons/.

"Diagnostic and Statistical Manual of Mental Disorders (DSM-5)." https://www.psychiatry.org/psychiatrists/practice/dsm.

Dion, M. R., et al. "Marriage and Relationship Skills Education as a Way to Prepare Prisoners for Reintegration." https://ideas.repec.org/p/mpr/mprres/b58bfb3119294770b8528eee37b4963d.html.

Dixon, Bruce. "Medical Neglect Stalks Georgia Prisons." https://www.commondreams.org/news/2011/01/05/medical-neglect-stalks-Georgia-prisons.

"Drug Courts: Special Feature." https://www.ojp.gov/feature/drug-courts/overview.

"DSM-IV Multiaxial System." https://web.archive.org/web/20100419111229/http://psyweb.com/Mdisord/DSM_IV/jsp/dsm_iv.jsp.

DuBois, W. E. B. *The Souls of Black Folk*. Edited by Henry Louis Gates Jr. and Terri Hume Oliver. Norton Critical Editions. New York: Norton, 1999.

Eckholm, Erik. "Inmates Report Mental Illness at High Levels." *New York Times*, September 7, 2006.

Eitzen, Stanley D., and Janis E. Johnston. *Inequality: Social Class and Its Consequences*. Boulder: Paradigm, 2007.

"Elmira." https://www.correctionhistory.org/html/chronicl/docs2day/Elmira.html.

Bibliography

Erickson, Patricia E., and Steven K. Erickson. *Crime, Punishment, and Mental Illness: Law and the Behavioral Sciences in Conflict.* New Brunswick: Rutgers University Press, 2008.

"Faith among Black Americans." https://pewforum.org/2021/2/16/faith-among-black-americans/.

Farabee, David, and Kevin Knight. *Treating Addicted Offenders: A Continuum of Effective Practices.* Kansas City: Civic Research Institute, 2004.

"Federal Judge Approves ACLU Settlement Forcing Sweeping Improvements in Conditions at Baltimore City Jail." https://www.aclu.org/press-releases/federal-judge-approves-aclu-settlement-forcing-sweeping-improvements-conditions.

Garland, Greg. "Contraband Floods Maryland Prisons." *The Baltimore Sun,* July 6, 2005.

Goldman, Robert M. Review of *Worse Than Slavery: Parchman Farm and the Ordeal of Jim Crow Justice* by David M. Oshinsky. *H-Net Reviews* (1997). https://networks.h-net.org/node/16794/reviews/16863/goldman-oshinsky-worse-slavery-parchman-farm-and-ordeal-jim-crow.

Graham, Lawrence Otis. *Our Kind of People: Inside America's Black Upper Class.* New York: HarperCollins, 2009.

"Guide to Records of the Department of Correctional Services.doc." http://www.archives.nysed.gov/common/archives/files/res_topics_legal_corrections.pdf.

"Heschel, Abraham Joshua." https://kinginstitute.stanford.edu/encyclopedia/heschel-abraham-joshua.

Hobbes, Thomas. *Leviathan.* Edited by Richard Tuck. Cambridge: Cambridge University Press, 1996.

Hyland, Tim. "City Jail Acupuncture Program in Doubt." *Baltimore Business Journal,* August 7, 2003.

"Incarcerated Women and Girls." https://www.sentencingproject.org/publications/incarcerated-women-and-girls/.

Kersting, Karen. "New Hope For Sex Offender Treatment." *American Psychological Association* 34.7 (2003) 52.

Lebacqz, Karen. *Six Theories of Justice: Perspectives from Philosophical and Theological Ethics.* Minneapolis: Augsburg, 1986.

LeBlanc, Adrian N. "Prison Is a Member of Their Family." *New York Times,* January 12, 2003. https://www.nytimes.com/2003/01/12/magazine/prison-is-a-member-of-their-family.html.

Locke, John. *The Second Treatise of Government.* Edited by Thomas P. Peardon. London: Pearson, 1952.

Losel, Friedrich, et al. "On the Effectiveness of Sexual Offender Treatment in Prisons: A Comparison of Two Different Evaluation Designs in Routine Practice." *SAGE Journals* 32.4 (2020) 452–75.

Losen, Daniel F., and Johanna Wald. *Deconstructing the School-to-Prison Pipeline: New Directions For Youth Development.* San Francisco: Jossey-Bass, 2003.

Bibliography

"Methadone." https://www.SAMHSA.gov/medication-assisted-treatment/medications-counseling-related-conditions/methadone#.

Metzner, Jeffrey L., and Jamie Fellner. "Solitary Confinement and Mental Illness in U.S. Prisons: A Challenge for Medical Ethics." *The Journal of the American Academy of Psychiatry and the Law* 38.1 (2010) 104–8.

Miller, David. *Justice for Earthlings: Essays in Political Philosophy.* Cambridge: Cambridge University Press, 2013.

Morris, Herbert. "Persons and Punishment." In *Punishment and Rehabilitation*, edited by Jeffrie G. Murphy, 74–93. Belmont, CA: Wadsworth, 1995.

Murphy, Jeffrie G. *Punishment and Rehabilitation.* Belmont: Wadsworth, 1995.

Niebuhr, Reinhold. *Moral Man and Immoral Society: A Study in Ethics and Politics.* Rev. ed. Louisville: Westminster John Knox, 2001.

Nilsen, Sigurd R. "Poverty in America: Consequences for Individuals and the Economy." https://www.gao.gov/assets/gao-07-343t.pdf.

Nishar, Shivani. "The Legacy of Deinstitutionalization." https://mhanational.org/blog/legacy-deinstitutionalization.

Opderbeck, David W. *Law and Theology: Classic Questions and Contemporary Perspectives.* Minneapolis: Fortress, 2019.

"Overview of Drug Courts." https://nij.ojp.gov/topics/articles/overview-drug-courts.

Pardini, Dustin A. "Religious Faith and Spirituality in Substance Abuse Recovery: Determining the Mental Health Benefits." *Journal of Substance Abuse Treatment* 19.4 (2000) 347–54.

Polgar, Michael. "Deinstitutionalization." http://www.minddisorders.com/Br-Del/Deinstitutionalization.html.

Raboteau, Albert J. "A Hidden Wholeness: Thomas Merton and Martin Luther King, Jr." *Spirituality Today* 40 (1988) 80–95.

Rawls, John. *A Theory of Justice.* Cambridge: Harvard University Press, 1971.

Reynolds, Matt. "Private Prisons Are a Failed Experiment with 'Perverse and Immoral Incentives,' ABA House Says in Calling for Their End." https://www.abajournal.com/news/article/resolution-507-aba-house-of-delegates-calls-for-an-end-to-private-prison-contracts.

Rhodes, Lorna A. *Total Confinement: Madness and Reason in the Maximum Security Prison.* Berkeley: University of California Press, 2004.

Rosenberg, Alana, et al. "Comparing Black and White Drug Offenders: Implications for Racial Disparities in Criminal Justice and Reentry Policy and Programming." *Journal of Drug Issues* 47.1 (2017) 132–42.

Rousseau, Jean-Jacques. *Discourse on Inequality.* Translated by Franklin Philip. Oxford World's Classics. New York: Oxford University Press, 2009.

———. *A Discourse on the Origins of Inequality.* Translated by G. D. H. Cole. Overland Park: Digireads, 2018.

———. *The Social Contract.* Translated by Christopher Betts. Oxford World's Classics. New York: Oxford University Press, 1999.

Russell, Craig. *Alternatives to Prison: Rehabilitation and Other Programs.* Philadelphia: Mason Crest, 2007.

Bibliography

Saha, Riya, and Jessica Feierman. "Strip-Searching Children Is State-Imposed Trauma." *Human Rights Magazine*, October 12, 2021.

Satz, Debra, and Rob Reich. *Toward a Humanist Justice: The Political Philosophy of Susan Moller Okin*. New York: Oxford University Press, 2009.

"The Science of Evil: 'Bad Barrels' or 'Bad Apples' at Abu Ghraib?" https://www.religionlink.com/source-guides/the-science-of-evil-bad-barrels-or-bad-apples/.

Sentementes, Gus G. "Officers Indicted in Death of Inmate: Smoot Was Killed in Melee in May at Baltimore's Central Booking." *The Baltimore Sun*, May 20, 2005.

Sheldon, Randall G. "Slavery in the Third Millennium Part II—Prisons and Convict Leasing Help Perpetuate Slavery." *The Black Commentator*, June 16, 2005. https://blackcommentator.com/142/142_slavery_2.html.

Shelton, Dinah, ed. *The Oxford Handbook of International Human Rights Law*. 1st ed. Oxford Handbooks. Oxford: Oxford University Press, 2013.

Silverstein, Ken. "US: America's Private Gulag." *Prison Legal News*, June 1, 2020. https://www.corpwatch.org/article/us-americas-private-gulag.

Simsbury Historical Society. "Newgate Prison." https://simsburyhistory.org/Simsbury-history-2/.

Sinden, Jeff. "The Problem of Prison Privatization: The US Experience." In *Capitalist Punishment: Prison Privatization & Human Rights*, edited by Andrew Coyle et al., 39–47. Atlanta: Clarity, 2003.

Smith, Roger. *Prison Conditions: Overcrowding, Disease, Violence, and Abuse*. Philadelphia: Mason Crest, 2015.

Spiegler, Michael D., and David C. Guevremont. *Contemporary Behavior Therapy*. Belmont: Wadsworth, 2010.

Steinhauer, Jennifer. "Studies Find Big Benefits in Marriage." *New York Times*, April 10, 1995.

Sullivan, Erin. "The Corrections: Inmates at the Baltimore Detention Center Want Out—But Until Then They'd Like Medical Care, Decent Food, and Humane Treatment." *Baltimore City Paper*, May 19, 2004.

Sweden, Josh. Review of *Theology of Work: Work in the New Creation*, by Darrell Cosden. Boston University School of Theology Center for Practical Theology. https://www.bu.edu/cpt/resources/book-reviews/theology-of-work-by-darrell-cosden/.

Szmigiera, M. "Countries with the Largest Number of Prisoners as of July 2021." https://www.statista.com/statistics/262961/countries-with-the-most-prisoners/.

"Thomas Mott Osborne: American Penologist." https://www.britannica.com/biography/Thomas-Mott-Osborne.

Tocqueville, Alexis de, and Henry Reeve. *Democracy in America*. Translated by Henry Reeve. New York: Bantam, 2000.

Todd, William Andrew. "Convict Lease System." https://www.georgiaencyclopedia.org/articles/history-archaeology/convict-lease-system.

Bibliography

United States Bureau of Prisons. *Handbook of Correctional Institution Design and Construction: A Source Book for Planning and Construction of Institutions Ranging in Type from the Small Jail and Short Term Detention Facilities for Juvenile Delinquents to the Maximum Security Type of Institution.* Washington, DC: United States Bureau of Prisons, 1949.

Welsh, Wayne N. "Multi-Site Evaluation of Prison-Based Drug Treatment: A Research Partnership between the Pennsylvania Department of Corrections and Temple University: Final Report." https://www.ojp.gov/ncjrs/virtual-library/abstracts/multi-site-evaluation-prison-based-drug-treatment-research.

"What Is the Difference between Dual Diagnosis vs Co-Occurring Disorders?" https://apibhs.com/2018/10/05/what-is-the-difference-between-dual-diagnosis-vs-co-occurring-disorders.

Wolterstorff, Nicholas. *Acting Liturgically: Philosophical Reflections on Religious Practice.* Oxford: Oxford University Press, 2018.

———. *Educating for Shalom: Essays on Christian Higher Education.* Edited by Clarence W. Joldersma and Gloria Goris Stronks. Grand Rapids: Erdmans, 2004.

Woodham, Chai. "Eastern State Penitentiary: A Prison with a Past. Philadelphia Set the Stage for Prison Reform Not Only in Pennsylvania, But Also the World Over." *Smithsonian Magazine*, September 30, 2008. https://smithsonianmag.com/history/eastern-state-penitentiary-a-prison-with-a-past-14274660/.

Index

Abu Ghraib, 94–95
abuse, of mentally ill offenders, 101–2
accountability, 107–8
ACLU National Prison Project, xxii, 100
Acting Liturgically (Wolterstorff), 27
acupuncture, 81
Adams, Chris, 84
Adams County Adult Correctional Complex, 16–17, 18, 89–90, 101–2, 105
addiction, xix–xx, 82, 83–84, 85–86, 87
Addicts Changing Together Substance Abuse Program (Baltimore City), 81
advocacy, within adjudication process, 78–79
African Americans
  addiction of, 83–84
  branding of, 66
  double consciousness and, 55
  family dissolution of, 79–80
  incarceration as rite of passage to, 50
  within jails/prisons, 73
  male figure absence within, 79–80
  railroads and, 50–51
  religious institutions and, 78
  suspicions regarding, 73
Alighieri, Dante, 52
Alternative Sentencing Commission, 117–18
Alternatives to Prison (Russell), 38
Amnesty International USA, xxii, 100
Anarchy, State, and Utopia (Nozick), 29
animals, fixed behaviors of, 64, 65
Arendt, Hannah, 15
art imitating life, 54
Auburn Prison, 42–43
Aucoin, Brent, 53

Baltimore City Detention Center, 14, 81
Baltimore City Public School #370, 89–90
banality of evil, 15
Barth, Karl, 3–4, 60, 67
Basis of Equality, 36
Beatitudes, 77
Beaumont, Gustave de, 39
Bertram, Chris, 64–65
bias, 37
Bible, legal material within, 5
Bivens, Donna, 54–55
Black church, xxiv, 78, 117
black market, within correctional facilities, 10
Blakinger, Keri, 111

127

Index

Blankenship, Kim, 83
Blitzman, Jay, 51
Bonhoeffer, Dietrich, 67
Bush, George W., 107

Calvin, John, 67
Campbell, Allison, 56
capacity for moral personality, xvii, xxii, 31–32
Capitalist Punishment, 56, 57
capital punishment, xx, 43, 95
Cavanaugh, Maureen, 50–51
cell extraction, 11
cell insertion, 11
Chao, Rex, 90
children, 75, 89
choice, 64–65, 70
Christianity, 27–28, 77
Church Dogmatics (Barth), 60
The Church Must Stand for Social Justice (Barth), 3–4
civic organizations, influence of, 117
civilization, character of, 27
classification system of inmates, 42
Code of Hammurabi, 62
cohabitating relationships, 80
Cole, G. H. D., 52–53, 65
Cole, Tim, 48
Coles, Roberta L., 79–80
community
  evidence based collaborations within, xix, 76–77, 78
  influence of, xix, 71–72
  responsibilities of, xxiii–xxiv
  role of, 117
community corrections, 117
community service programs, 118
compassion, 4, 15
condoms, 109
Conjectures of a Guilty Bystander (Merton), 4–5

Contemporary Behavior Therapy (Spiegler and Guevremont), 19
contractarianism, 60
convict lease system, 48–50, 51, 55
co-occurring disorders, 20–21
correctional facilities
  . *See* jails/prisons
correctional officers
  adversarial relationships of, 104–5
  aggression by, 12
  black market entrepreneurship by, 10
  complicity of, 9
  corruption of, 10
  fraternization by, 11
  jail/prison conditions and, 114–15
  murder by, 11–12
  punitive measures regarding, xxii–xxiii
  rape and, 108
  role of, 9
  suicide and, 113–14
  tenure of, 104
Corrections Corporation of America (CoreCivic), 47–48, 56, 57, 111
Cosden, Darrell, 67
Coyle, Andrew, 56
Crime, Punishment and Mental Illness (Erickson and Erickson), 93
Cullen, Francis T., 117

Dahmer, Jeffrey, 93
Dakwar, Jamil, 119
Davis, Angela, 30–31, 120
Day, Dorothy, 70–71
day reporting center program, 118
death notifications, 11–12, 14–15
Declaration of Independence, 61
deferred sentencing programs, 118

Index

defund the police movement, 31
deinstitutionalization, 100
Democracy in America (Tocqueville), 38–39
Dickens, Charles, 44
difference principle, xv–xvi, 35, 36
disciplinary boards, 37
A Discourse for the Academy of Dijon (Cole), 65
Discourse on the Origins of Inequality (Rousseau), 65
diversion programs, 118
Division of Pretrial Detention and Services, 86
Dixon, Bruce A., 111
double consciousness, 55
Draughon, Mr., 11
drug courts, xx, 87–88, 118
DSM-IV Diagnostic and Statistical Manual of Mental Disorders, 7, 19–20
dual diagnosis, 20, 23
Du Bois, W. E. B., xxiv–xxv, 55, 118–19

East Baltimore, jails/prisons within, 75–76
Eastern State Penitentiary, 43–45
Eckholm, Erik, 101
Educating for Shalom (Wolterstorff), 2
education
 of correctional officers, 104
 as incarceration factor, 88–89
 within inmate treatment plans, xiv, 18
 within jails/prisons, 89–90
 poverty and, 90–91
 statistics regarding, 83, 90
Eitzen, Stanley, 65–66
electric chair, 42, 43
electronic monitoring programs, 118
Elmira Reformatory (Elmira, New York), 45–46

employment, as moral imperative, 67
environment, influence of, xix
Epstein, Joseph, 39
equality, as justice, 36
Erickson, Patricia E., 93
Erickson, Steven K., 93
essential character, 59, 60, 61–62
ethics, 34, 37, 97–98
evil, xx, 93, 94–95
execution(s), 42, 43
ex-offenders, 16–17, 66–67

family/family structures, 16–18, 72, 78–80, 84
Farabee, David, 85
fathers, absence of, 79–80
Feierman, Jessica, 8–9
Fellner, Jamie, 102
fellow feeling, 15
female offenders, 115
Finn, Pat, 50–51
fog of war, 64
for-profit jails/prisons, xvi, xvii, 46–58
Fort Leavenworth Detention Barracks, 32–33
Franklin, Benjamin, 46
fraternization, 11
free will, sex offenders and, 97

Gacy, John Wayne, 93
Garland, Greg, 10
Gates, Louis, 73
Gazis-Sax, Joel, 41
Geo Group (Wackenhut Corrections), 56, 57–58
Gettysburg College, 90
Girl Scouts Beyond Bars, 18
glamorization of incarceration, 53–54
Global Assessment of Functioning (GAF), 20, 23
goals, within corrections ethics, xv, 30–32

Index

Goldman, Robert M., 52
Graham, Lawrence Otis, 74
Green, Charles, 80
Groves, Allison, 83
Guevremont, David C., 19

hard labor, as rehabilitation, 42
Hardwood, Robert J., Jr., 90
Helling v. McKinney, 13–14
heroin, 84, 85–86
Heschel, Abraham Joshua, 4
HIV/AIDS, 86, 107, 108–9
Hobbes, Thomas, 1, 60, 62, 106
home detention, 118
homeless population, 101
hooding, 43
humane treatment of inmates, 13
human rights, 30, 61, 67

inalienable natural rights, 59
inconvenience, enacting of, 62
Individual's Right to Petition the United Nations, xxiv–xxv, 118–19
Inequality (Eitzen, Johnston, and Riemann), 65–66
The Inferno (Alighieri), 52
injustice, 35, 93
inmates
    classification system of, 42
    as commodities, xvii, 57–58
    disciplinary boards and, 37
    empowerment of, xvi, 35–36
    family of, 74
    humane treatment of, 13
    individuality of, xiv, xvii, 24–25
    manipulation by, 106
    mothers as, 18
    neglect of, 18
    power generated from, 40
    rehabilitation capabilities of, xvii–xviii
    right to life for, xx–xxi
    as scattered individuals, xv, 32–33, 92, 94
    segregation of, 43, 44
    self-worth of, 106
    weapons of, 14
inmate treatment plans, xiv, 18
intensive probation supervision (IPS) program, 118
internalized racist oppression, xvi, 54–55
Islam, 27
isolation, 41
    . *See also* solitary confinement
Isom, Jessica, 83–84

jail/prison reform, xiii–xiv, 13
jails/prisons
    abolition of, 30–31
    abuse of power within, 34–35
    alternatives to, 104–20
    black market within, 10
    culture of, xxii–xxiii
    debilitating conditions within, 8–9
    as de facto universities, 78
    defined, 38
    demographics of, 36–37, 65
    history of, 38–46
    humane ethics within, 26
    isolation of, 37–38
    location impact of, 75–76
    power disproporationality within, xv
    profit reception regarding, xxi–xxii
    public perception of, 37
    rules interpretation within, 36
    transparency within, xxiii
Jefferson, Thomas, 61
Jesus, 27
John Paul II, 67
Johns Hopkins University, 90
Johnson, Cheryl Lero, 117
Johnston, Janis E., 65–66
Judaism, 27
justice
    equality as, 36

Index

as fairness, 30
moral reasoning regarding, 3
within Old Testament literature, 2, 3
principles of, 27, 67–68
public conception of, 29
as social institution virtue, 2
within social systems, 35
understanding of, 29
just society, 98
juvenile offenders, 8–9, 115, 116

Kant, Immanuel, 3, 60
Kemmler, William, 42
Kersting, Karen, 96–97
Knight, Kevin, 85

law, 5, 6
Law and Theology (Opderbeck), 2–3, 5
Lebacqz, Karen, 35
LeBlanc, Adrian Nicole, 76
legacy correctional institutionalization, 74–75, 78
The Leviathan (Hobbes), 62
Lex Talionis (Law of Retaliation), 62
life imitating art, 54
Lincoln Intermediate School (Gettysburg, Pennsylvania), 90
Locke, John, 1, 30, 60–61
lockstep, 42
Luther, Martin, 67

Mala in Se, 15
Malvo, Lee Boyd, 75
manipulation, 106
marijuana, 10–11
marriage, benefits of, 80–81
Marx, Karl, 67
Maryland Correctional Enterprises (State Use Industries), 49, 55

Maryland Division of Pretrial Detention and Services, 10, 11–12, 75, 89–90, 110, 113
maximin, xxi, 99
Mears, Daniel P., 117
medical clinics/facilities, transparency within, xxiii, 112
medical malpractice, xxiii, 109–11
mental health, 19, 20–21
mentally ill offenders/mental illness, xxii, 100, 101–2, 103
Merton, Thomas, 4–5
methadone, 85–86
Metzner, Jeffrey L., 102
morality of association, xix, 71–72, 88
morality of authority, 71, 75, 79
Moral Man and Immoral Society (Niebuhr), 3
moral personality, 59, 92, 94
moral shame, 114
Morris, Herbert, 63
mothers, as inmates, 18
move, defined, 60
murder, 11–12
Murphy, Jeffries G., 63
music, 53, 54
mutual benefit, 68–69
The Myth of the Black Father (Coles and Green), 80

NAACP, 118–19
National Commission on Correctional Health Care, 111
natural assets, xv, 24–25
natural law, 6
natural rights, 30, 67
Neufeld, Rodney, 56
Newgate Prison (Simsbury, Connecticut), 39–40
New Testament, law and justice within, 5
The New York Times, 76
Niebuhr, Reinhold, 3, 34–35, 77
nodding, 86

Index

nonprofit organizations, influence of, 117
Nozick, Robert, 29

Office of the United Nations High Commissioner for Human Rights, 119
Okin, Susan, 17–18
Oklahoma Marriage Initiative, 82
Old Testament, justice theme within, 2, 3
Olsen, Daniel J., 90
On Poverty (Day), 70–71
Opderbeck, David W., 2–3, 5, 6
opportunity, environment of, 67–68
oppression, of racism, xvi, 54–55
original position, 57, 98, 99–100
Osborne, Thomas Mott, 46
Oshinsky, David M., 52
The Other, 4
Our Kind of People (Graham), 74

Paine, Thomas, 29–30
Parchman Farm (Mississippi), 52, 53, 55
Paul, writings of, 5
Paul and Silas Alternative Sentencing Initiative (PASASI), xxiv, 117–18
penitentiary, 41
Pennsylvania Prison Society, xxii, 37, 46, 100
Pennsylvania System, 41, 42, 44–45
Philadelphia Society for Alleviating the Miseries of Public Prisons, 46
policies, transparency of, 112
Porter, Arnold, 111
poverty, 65, 70, 90–91
power, 34–35, 40
primary goods, xviii, 66, 68, 111–12
principles of justice, 27

Prison Conditions (Smith), 107
prison industrial complex, business model within, 55
Prison Rape Elimination Act, 107
Prison Reform (Gazis-Sax), 41
prisons
. *See* jails/prisons
prison songs, 53
Prison Watch Network, xxii, 100
private jails/prisons, xvi, 46–58
property crimes, 84
prostitution, 84
psychological breaking of the inmate, 52–53
punishment, xvii, 63–64
Punishment and Rehabilitation (Murphy), 63

Quakers, 41

racialized communities, erosion of, xviii, 69
racism, xvi, 54–55
railroads, 50–51
Ramirez, Richard, 93–94
rape, jail/prison, xxii–xxiii, 107–9
rap music, 54
Rawls, John
 influence of, 2
 quote of, xiv, xviii, 2, 16, 24–25, 36, 45, 51, 58, 68, 71, 93, 98, 111–12, 114
 social contract theory of, 26–33, 60–61, 62, 71
 viewpoint of, xv, 60, 84, 99, 120
recidivism, 16–17
reflective equilibrium, xiv, 16
rehabilitation programming
 capabilities within, 64
 capital punishment *versus*, xx
 empowerment through, xvi, 35–36
 examples of, xvii–xviii
 labor/hard labor as, 40, 42
religion, 27, 86–87

Index

religious institutions, 78, 117
restorative justice, 118
Reynolds, Matt, 47
Rhodes, Lorna A., 113
Rhodes v. Chapman, 13–14
Riemann, Jeffrey, 65–66
Rights of Man (Paine), 29–30
right to life, 95
right to petition, xxiv–xxv
Robert, story of, 21–24
Rosenberg, Alana, 83
Rousseau, Jean-Jacques, xvi, 1, 53, 54, 60, 64–65
Russell, Craig, 38

Saha, Riya, 8–9
scattered individuals, xv, 32–33, 92, 94
Schaefer, Kevin, 90
school-to-prison pipeline (STPP), 51
Second Treatise of Government (Locke), 30, 61
security, 113, 114
security personnel, xxiii, 112–14
segregation, 43, 44, 115
self-respect, 112
self-worth, 106
Sellin, Thorsten, 49
Sentementes, Gus G., 12
Sermon on the Mount, 5
sex offenders, xxi, 95–98
sexual abuse, 11
Sheldon, Randall G., 49–50
Silverstein, Emily, 90
Silverstein, Ken, 47–48
Simsbury Historical Society, 39, 40
Sinden, Jeff, 56, 57
single-cell construction, 42, 43
situation factors and social dynamics, xx
Six Theories of Justice (Lebacqz), 35
slavery, 48–49, 51, 52–53

Smith, Roger, 107
Smoot, Raymond K., 11–12
sober living environment programs, 118
soboxone, 86
The Social Contract (Rousseau), 64
The Social Contract or Principles of Political Right (Cole), 52–53
social contract theory, 26–33, 60–61, 62, 71
social institutions, xv, 2, 17
social stratification, xviii
social systems, 35
societal norms, xix
solitary confinement, 8, 41, 102
Solitary Watch, xxii, 100
The Souls of Black Folk (Du Bois), 55
Special Emergency Response Team (SERT), 21–22
Spiegler, Michael D., 19
spirituality, as treatment component, 86–87
Stanford Encyclopedia of Philosophy, 64–65
state of nature, 60, 106–7
State Use Industries (Maryland Correctional Enterprises), 49, 55
Steinhauer, Jennifer, 80–81
Stemple, Lara, 107
stepping mill, 40
Stewart, Mary, 81
Stinney, George, Jr., 43
Strawn, Brent, 5
strip-searching, 8–9
succession of generations, xviii–xix, 71, 74
suffering, 27–28
suicide, 113–15
Sullivan, Erin, 14
sympatheia, 15

tabula rosa, 72
Taylor, William Banks, 53

Index

tenure, of correctional officers, 104
terrorism, capital punishment as, 43
Theology of Work (Cosden), 67
A Theory of Justice (Rawls)
  difference principle within, 35
  quote within, 2, 16, 24–25, 29, 31–32, 36, 51, 58, 71, 72
therapeutic community (TC) model, xix, 85
Thirteen Turns, 82–83
Till, Emmett Louis, 12
tobacco, black market regarding, 10
Tocqueville, Alexis de, 38–39, 42
Torah, 5
torture, 40
Total Confinement (Rhodes), 113
Towns, Edolphus, 48
transcarceration, 101
treadmill, 40
tread wheel, 40
Treating Addicted Offenders (Knight and Farabee), 85
treatment, xvii, 22–24, 63–64, 113. *See also specific treatments*
treatment plan, 21–22
treatment professionals/staff, xxiii, 21, 105

Ulpian, 2–3
unemployment, of ex-offenders, 66–67
uniforms, 42
United Nations, Individual's Right to Petition, xxiv–xxv, 118–19
United Nations Human Rights, 13
United Nations Standard Minimum Rules for the Treatment of Prisoners, xxii, 100
United States, incarceration statistics of, 7–8
Universal Declaration of Human Rights, 13, 66
upward mobility, exclusion from, 66

veil of ignorance, xxi, 57, 98, 99
Violent Crime Control Act, 48
Volf, Miroslav, 67

Wackenhut Corrections (Geo Group), 56, 57–58
Wald, Johanna, 90
Walnut Street Jail, 40–41
Walte, Linda, 80–81
wealth, hoarding of, 68–69
weapons, 14
weekend jail programs, 118
Welsh, Wayne N., 85
Wheeler Correctional Facility, 111
Wolterstorff, Nicholas, 2, 27
Woodham, Chai, 44
Wordsworth Academy (Harrisburg, Pennsylvania), 89
work, as moral imperative, 67
work release programs, 118
Worse Than Slavery (Goldman), 52

Zeigler, Tillie, 42
Zimbardo, Philip, xx, 94–95

www.ingramcontent.com/pod-product-compliance
Lightning Source LLC
Chambersburg PA
CBHW051109160426
43193CB00010B/1375